POPE JOHN PAUL II

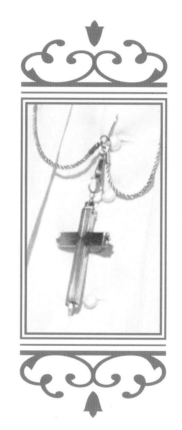

POPE JOHN PAUL II

Jo Garcia-Cobb

MetroBooks

MetroBooks

An Imprint of Friedman/Fairfax Publishers

©1999 by Michael Friedman Publishing Group, Inc.

Library of Congress Cataloging-in-Publication Data

Garcia-Cobb, Jo.
    Pope John Paul II / Jo Garcia-Cobb
       p.   cm.
    Includes bibliographical references and index.
    ISBN 1-56799-827-5
    1. John Paul II, Pope, 1920– . 2. Popes Biography. I. Title.
  II. Title: Pope John Paul 2. III. Title: Pope John Paul the Second.
BX1378.5.G37   1999
282′.092—dc21
[B]   99-39621
                                             CIP

Editor: Ann Kirby
Art Director: Jeff Batzli
Designer: Meredith Miller
Photography Editor: Jennifer Bove/Erin Feller
Production Manager: Richela Fabian

Color separations by Fine Arts Repro House Co., Ltd.
Printed in Hong Kong by Sing Cheong Printing Company Ltd.

1 3 5 7 9 10 8 6 4 2

For bulk purchases and special sales, please contact:
Friedman/Fairfax Publishers
Attention: Sales Department
15 West 26th Street
New York, NY 10010
212/685-6610   FAX 212/685-1307

Visit our website:
www.metrobooks.com

Dedication

Dedicated to my parents, Jaime and Remedios Garcia, and my parents-in-law, Kenneth and Geneva Cobb, who, next to God, make all things possible; and to all those who are building bridges of peace between the world's religions.

Acknowledgments

My love and gratitude goes to my husband, Keith Ellis Cobb, who wouldn't let me do house chores while I was writing this book. His intelligence, patience, and support helped birth this book.

Thanks also to the people at The Michael Friedman Publishing Group who pulled this book together: Ann Kirby, my editor, a dynamo and a joy to work with, whose enthusiasm, trust, and generous appreciation made writing this book as fun and as painless as possible; Karen Matsu Greenberg, production director, who first envisioned a book on Pope John Paul II; Jennifer Bove, photography editor, for putting together a rich harvest of images from the pope's life; Meredith Miller, for the elegant design; Richela Fabian, for meticulously seeing the book through the production process; Andrea Karman, for the lovely jacket design; and Don Kennison, copyeditor, for catching errors no one else sees.

For aiding my research, I am indebted to: Fr. Adam Barcz, Ewa Kolodziejczyk, Leonard Zawazki, and Lech Kiszynski for helping me navigate Polish history and Polish spelling; Fr. Anthony Rosevear, O.P.; Fr. Raymond Finerty, O.P.; Fr. Brendan McAnerney, O.P., and Rev. Mr. Arthur Anderson for deeply enriching my knowledge of the Catholic faith; Prakash Chenjeri, PhD, professor of philosophy at Southern Oregon University, for his course in Philosophy of Religion, and for loaning me books that helped me grasp the significance of Pope John Paul II's work in global interfaith dialogue; and Anna Sienkiewicz, MA, head of the research information department at the Jagiellonian University in Kraków, Poland, for her patience in digging up hard-to-find information.

CONTENTS

From Poet to Pope

Spiritual leader of more than one billion faithful. World statesman. Relentless spokesperson for peace, human rights, and universal values. The man whose moral force helped end the Cold War and redraw the political map of Europe through nonviolent resistance. A visionary whose battles with the deepest crises of our time have defined our age as has no other world leader.

The story of Karol Josef Wojtyla has touched and inspired countless lives. From humble beginnings in Poland, he rose to become pontiff of the Roman Catholic Church. His tireless efforts to create peace among nations and religions, and to work for a more just and equitable world, have created a watershed, "a threshold of hope," that he asks others to cross with courage.

As a young man, he lived through the horrors of World War II, barely escaping arrest and death. He was a laborer, a poet, an actor, a playwright, and a philosopher. As priest, he lived and preached his faith in a totalitarian and atheistic regime. As pope, he has shown the world how to face the great challenges of our time with faith and with love.

CHAPTER ONE
Beginnings

A Slavic Pope

In time of quarrels God will choose
A Slavic pope, braver than the Italian
Who came before him. He will be unafraid
To take on a fight.

His face shining, his power
Will stop the whirling sun;
His word will lead the nations
Into purest light.

He is coming! The blood in our veins
Will quicken! Spirit is power.
His Spirit-Power will turn the Earth.
The Folk-Pope salves our wounds.

Angels strew his throne with lilies;
He gives love where the mighty give arms.
He bestows the strength of sacrament.
A dove flies out from his song, giving hope.

The sky opens and nations make peace.
He sweeps clean the Church.
The Slavic Pope will come
To reveal God's hand in all creation.

—Juliusz Slowacki, 1866

his vision of a Slavic pope was written by one of Poland's most beloved poets, Juliusz Slowacki, more than fifty years before the birth of Karol Josef Wojtyla, the future Pope John Paul II. Like most Poles, Slowacki longed for lasting peace with an intensity known only to a people who, for centuries, had lived through war.

Slowacki's poem appeared in 1866, shortly after Poland had been overrun and partitioned a third time by her covetous neighbors—Russia, Prussia, and Austria—disappearing from the map for 125 years. To Slowacki, Poland was the "Christ of Nations," a nation that had undergone a journey not unlike Christ's— a journey through birth, death, and resurrection.

Poland, the Knight of Nations, had for centuries fought waves of invasion from the east, defending Western civilization and, with it, Christianity from the Huns, the Mongols, the Tartars, and the Turks. For this defense of Europe, as the historian Louis E. Van Norman wrote, "She asked no contributions of troops or money. She asked no thanks. The treatment she has actually received from Europe is one of the crimes of the ages."

Like the other Polish Romantic poets, Slowacki believed that each individual nation was an instrument of divine will to help humanity achieve lasting peace, based on justice, liberty, and charity, and what better contribution from Poland than a spiritual leader—a pope—who would serve this cause? Such a vision captured the Polish imagination so that even in her darkest moments Poland kept alive her poets' transcendent ideals. She never really lost touch with heaven. This, perhaps, was her most precious gift to the child who would be pope.

PAGE 10: *An undated photo of Karol Wojtyla as a young priest.*
PAGE 11: *A detail from John Paul II's papal robe. Karol Wojtyla had the letter "M" inscribed on his crest to symbolize his devotion to the Blessed Virgin Mary.*
LEFT: *Karol Josef Wojtyla, or "Lolek," after receiving his First Communion. Although raised in an atmosphere of strict religious observance, Lolek, as a child, showed no strong bent toward a religious calling.*

Mother

At the moment of Karol Josef's birth, on May 18, 1920, his mother, Emilia Kaczorowska Wojtyla, asked the midwife to open the window of the family's second-floor apartment. From the Our Lady of Perpetual Help Church across the street, hymns in honor of the Virgin Mary flooded the room. It was the month dedicated to Our Lady. Years later, long after the death of his own mother, Karol Josef Wojtyla would dedicate his priestly life to the Holy Virgin—the mother who would never leave him.

Early on, Emilia Kaczorowska Wojtyla sensed the offing of greatness in her midst. "You'll see, my Lolek (Karol Josef's nickname) will be a great man," she would tell friends. Undaunted by the pains of illness, poverty, and the burdens of war, Emilia was known to have a deep inner calm. Her big brown eyes, however, often spoke of lingering sorrow from the loss of her daughter, Olga, who died at birth, six years before Lolek was born.

Convent-bred Emilia was cheerful, charming, and deeply devoted to her family. Although stricken with a debilitating illness, she managed to help make ends meet by taking on sewing jobs. She took loving care of Lolek, with much help from her husband, Karol, whenever illness consigned her to bed. Lolek learned his first prayers and heard his first earful of Scripture from her. The first altar he knelt at was the one his mother had arranged in the parlor of their humble apartment.

On April 13, 1929, while her son was at school, Emilia died of heart and kidney inflammation at the age of forty-five. "It's God's will," Lolek is remembered as saying in stoic fashion after learning about his mother's death. Years later, however, the depth of his grief would surface when, at the age of nineteen, he memorialized her in a poem.

ABOVE: *Portrait of a young Lolek. He resembled his mother, with his broad facial planes, more than his father. The loss of his mother at an early age may help explain Karol's special devotion to the Virgin Mary.*
OPPOSITE: *Father Edward Zacher was Karol's religion teacher at the Wadowice Gymnasium. (In Poland, a gymnasium is a preparatory school for college.) Lolek's parents sent him to a public school, rather than a parochial one, because they believed that a public school would provide a more eclectic classical education.*

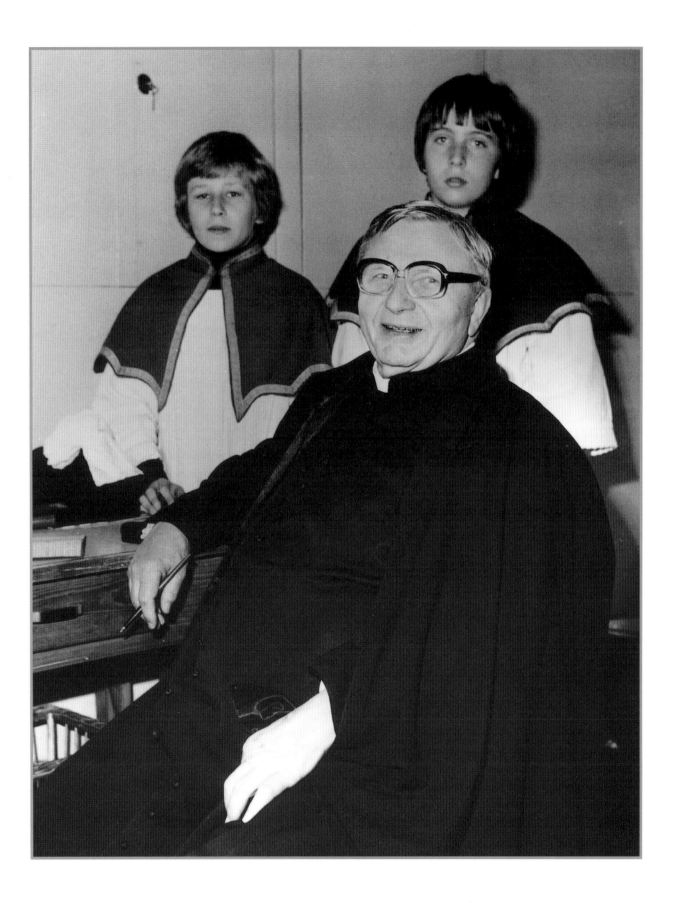

Brother

dmund (nicknamed Mundek) was Lolek's hero. Fourteen years Lolek's senior, Mundek was an honor student, a soccer star, and a fine bridge and chess player. Through Lolek's school years, Mundek was away, studying medicine at the Jagiellonian University in Kraków. He was a constant visitor in Wadowice, however, where he often took his little brother hiking, skiing, and to soccer games.

Mundek inspired in Lolek a great love of the outdoors, a passion that Lolek, as a priest ministering to youths, also passed on to his students. Lolek and his students frequently swam, hiked, and skied their

way to knowledge. The brothers also shared a passion for drama, staging mini-theatrical acts for Mundek's patients at the hospital where he worked, as Lolek's acting career began to bud in school.

Tragically, on December 5, 1932, two years after graduating from medical school, Edmund died of scarlet fever, a disease he had contracted from a patient. Mundek's death was a terrible blow to Lolek. And yet, as with his mother's death, Lolek remarked: "It's God's will."

OPPOSITE, TOP: *Lolek (back row, far left) with classmates at the Wadowice Gymnasium. Karol senior and Lolek often invited Lolek's friends to their home, where Karol senior read books on Polish history and literature to Lolek and his friends.*

OPPOSITE, BOTTOM: *Karol's report card, when he was seventeen, covering his first-term work. During prewar education in Poland, students received four marks: "very good," "good," "satisfactory," and "unsatisfactory." In religion, Polish, Latin, Greek, German, math, philosophy, and physical education, Karol earned a "very good" mark. In history, chemistry, and physics, Karol received a "good" mark. At this time, Karol was bent on studying Polish philology and literature in college.*

ABOVE: *The E. Zygadlowicz Gymnasium in Wadowice, founded in 1866, where Karol received his graduation certificate in pre-university preparatory education.*

Father

Having lost his mother at a tender age, almost all of Karol Josef Wojtyla's memories from childhood and adolescence are associated with his father.

Karol senior, a retired army lieutenant, and Karol junior were kindred souls. The father who, in John Paul II's words, "didn't have to demand anything of his son," had in fact, a son who didn't have to demand anything of his father. Karol senior's deep prayer life, his love of knowledge, and his penchant for regimen found a happy consort in his son. Lolek found no reason to complain about his prescribed daily routine: Mass in the morning, school, play, Mass in the afternoon, homework, and leisurely strolls in the evening with his father.

After Emilia's death, Karol senior performed the roles of both father and mother to his two sons. As Lolek's elder brother, Edmund, was studying medicine in Kraków, Lolek and his father were left by themselves, a constant twosome. Karol senior cooked, sewed Lolek's clothes, and by his own pious life, laid the foundations of Lolek's future vocation. Father and son slept in one bedroom; they ate, prayed, read, and played together.

After his wife's death, Karol senior became socially withdrawn and given to long, reflective prayer. Lolek would often wake up in the middle of the night and see his father prostrate at their altar. In one of his most revealing interviews, the pope told French journalist André Frossard, "The violence of the blows that struck my father opened up immense spiritual depths in him. . . . The mere fact of seeing him on his knees had a decisive influence on my early years."

To the Wojtylas, as to most Catholic Poles, religion was a way of life rooted in the thousand-year history of Roman Catholicism in Poland. Religiously, Karol senior took Lolek on pilgrimages to

the Kalwaria Zebrzydowska, a Bernardine monastery thirty miles (48km) from their hometown of Wadowice, where tens of thousands of pilgrims gathered at Easter to witness the reenactment of the death and resurrection of Christ. In August, Karol senior and Lolek would go to Kalwaria to participate in the feast of the Assumption of Our Lady, the Virgin Mary's ascent into heaven. The Wojtylas' home was an extension of their church: religious artwork on the walls, the well-used altar, and a font of holy water by the door.

In the winter of 1940, a few years after Karol junior and he moved to Kraków, Karol senior became seriously ill. On the evening of February 18, 1941, while Karol junior was out getting his father's medicine, Karol senior died of a heart attack. That night Karol, in tears, cried out to a friend, "I wasn't there when my mother died. I wasn't there when my brother died. I wasn't there when my father died." Recalling the night of his father's death, John Paul II said, "I had never felt so alone." Only twenty-two years old, Karol had lost all his family.

OPPOSITE: *An undated photo of Karol Sr. and Emilia Wojtyla with child Lolek. The seeds of faith that Lolek's parents gave him were to grow and multiply.*
RIGHT: *The Church of Our Lady of Perpetual Help in Wadowice, where Karol Wojtyla was baptized.*

Karol Josef Wojtyla spent the first eighteen years of his life in Wadowice, a small town of seven thousand people nestled in the foothills of the Beskid Mountains, forty miles (64km) southwest of Poland's cultural capital, Kraków.

Like Kraków, Wadowice had a vibrant cultural life and excellent public schools. It had nearly as many public libraries—three of them—as it had factories, as well as several auditoriums for both amateur and professional theater.

John Paul II's brilliant command of the classics, his passion for Polish philology and literature, and his undying interest in astrophysics and cosmology date back to his high school days in Wadowice. By the time he graduated from high school, Karol was fluent in Latin and Greek; a quarter of a century later, he would stun the Second Vatican Council with his flawless Latin.

Founded in 1327, Wadowice had evolved into something of a capital for surrounding villages. Its population was a mix of peasants, professionals, artisans, intellectuals, laborers, priests, monks, nuns, rabbis, shopkeepers, artists, and officers and soldiers of the town garrison. The spire and cupola of the Church of Our Lady of Perpetual Help dominated Wadowice's landscape. The Wojtylas lived across the street from the church, at 2 Rynek Street, a second-floor two-bedroom apartment owned by Chaim Balamuth. A Jew, Balamuth operated a crystal and glassware shop on the ground floor, below the Wojtyla apartment.

Although predominantly Catholic, Wadowice had a Jewish population of more than 1,200, with a synagogue and a Jewish cemetery, which were later destroyed by the Nazis during World War II. Until the late 1930s, Jews worked as lawyers, doctors, dentists, and merchants without conflict alongside Christians.

"I can vividly remember the Jews who gathered every Saturday at the synagogue behind our school," recalled Pope John Paul II,

LEFT: *The foothills of the Carpathian Mountain Range, which includes the Beskid Mountains, were home to people from all walks of life. The local peasants' simple way of life inspired many of Karol's earlier poems.*
OPPOSITE: *A tourist photographs the plaque marking the birthplace of Pope John Paul II. The Wojtylas lived here until Karol and his father moved to Kraków for Karol to attend the Jagiellonian University.*

many years later. "Both religious groups, Catholics and Jews, were united, I presume, by the awareness that they prayed to the same God."

As the Third Reich began to actively breed anti-Semitism in Germany and neighboring countries, some Jewish Poles decided to leave Poland. The Beers, Jewish friends and neighbors of the Wojtylas', decided that they should send their daughter, Ginka, to Palestine, where they would later follow.

The former Ginka Beer, now Regina Reisenfeld, told journalists at her home in Israel, "We decided to leave Poland for Palestine because we felt disaster faced the Jews. . . . I went to say good-bye to Lolek and his father. Mr. Wojtyla was upset about our departure, and when he asked me why, I told him. Again and again he said to me, 'Not all Poles are anti-Semitic. You know I am not!'. . . He was very upset. But Lolek was even more upset than his father. He did not say a word, but his face became very red. I said farewell to him as kindly as I could, but he was so moved that he could not find a single word in reply. So I just shook his father's hand and left."

Many of Lolek's dearest friends, both Jews and Christians, perished during the Nazi occupation of Poland. The Holocaust would haunt him for the rest of his life and fire his zeal to help create a world free from hatred.

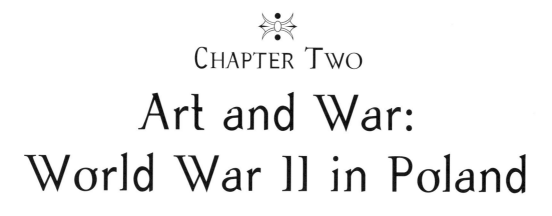

CHAPTER TWO

Art and War: World War II in Poland

The Word and the Actor

In May 1938, Karol entered Jagiellonian University in Krakow to study Polish philology and literature. Founded in 1364, the Jagiellonian had become by the middle of the fifteenth century a major center of learning in Europe, an Eden for new ideas in science and philosophy. It was here that Nicolaus Copernicus (1473–1543) shook the foundations of scientific thought when he theorized that the earth was not the center of the universe.

Karol had finished his first year of study when World War II broke out. While closing down all educational institutions in German-occupied Poland, the Nazis rounded up more than two hundred of the Jagiellonian's professors, many of whom died in the Sachsenshausen concentration camp.

Despite the closing of the Jagiellonian, Karol's love of literature continued to flourish in the Polish underground theater. After a brief stint with a semiprofessional theater group called Studio 39, Karol joined Miezyslaw Kotlarczyk's Rhapsodic Theater Company. The Rhapsodists conducted their activities in strict secrecy, at the risk of arrest and execution. Kotlarczyk reminisces, "Those Wednesdays and Saturdays were unforgettable, despite terror and arrests. The rehearsals of works by the great Polish poets went on, often in a dark, cold kitchen, sometimes with just a candle or two. But we firmly believed in our survival; we were sure we would reach the frontiers of freedom . . ."

The Rhapsodic Theater was, as Kotlarczyk put it, an artistic experiment, a "listening to rather than watching for . . . spectacle, a theater of the *word*." The company had conceived the Theater of the Living Word, which a theater critic, Maria Bojarska, referred to as "a theater of imagination, a theater of the inner self." In it, theater was stripped to its bare essentials; scenery was kept to a minimum. Emphasis was made on the delivery of the poetic text.

"Let theater be a church where the national spirit will flourish," the nineteen-year-old Karol wrote to Kotlarczyk in 1939. The Theater of the Living Word, in a sense, was a collective spiritual exercise. In keeping with the ideals of the Polish Romantic poets, it confronted fundamental problems and questions of human existence and plumbed the depths of language as an authentic expression of the soul.

ABOVE: *Entrance to Auschwitz II, better known as the Birkenau ("Brzezinka" in Polish) concentration camp. It is now a vast complex of ruins left exactly as it was the day the Nazis blew it up to destroy evidence of their crimes. Karol could have been arrested any day and taken to a concentration camp.*

The realities of the war made the exercise of the Theater of the Living Word more precise, as theater was reduced to what the company perceived to be its essence. Karol later wrote, "The unheard-of scarcity of the means of expression turned into a creative experiment. The company discovered . . . that the fundamental element of dramatic art is the living human word. It is the nucleus of drama, a leaven through which human deeds pass and from which they derive their proper dynamics."

Karol took part in all of the seven wartime productions of the Rhapsodic Theater—that is, in twenty-two performances and over a hundred rehearsals, all clandestine. His performances dazzled his peers for their depth and sensitivity. Other members of the company were convinced that Karol's future was in the theater.

In addition to acting, Karol wrote three plays between 1940 and 1941—*Job*, *Jeremiah*, and *David*—all of which dealt with Poland's dark night of the soul. The end of this period, he exhorted, would have to come, not by defending Poland with the sword, but through spiritual renewal.

After starring in Rhapsodic Theater productions in the winter of 1943, Karol asked Kotlarczyk not to cast him in future productions. Karol had decided to enter the seminary and become a priest. Karol's decision came as a shock to Kotlarczyk and the rest of the Rhapsodists. They tried to dissuade Karol from quitting, but to no avail. Karol said later, "Mr. Miezyslaw Kotlarczyk thought that my vocation would be in language and theater, while the Lord Jesus thought that it would be priesthood, and somehow we agreed on this."

ABOVE: *Young Karol Wojtyla gave up acting in 1943 to heed his calling to the priesthood.*
PAGE 22: *An undated photo of Fr. Karol Wojtyla.*
PAGE 23: Christ Appearing to Saint Peter on the Appian Way.
Annibale Carracci, c. 1601–1602. The National Gallery, London.

Poland's Dark Night

As one historian remarked, nothing happening in Poland today makes sense without reference to the nation's tortured history, particularly the grim legacy of World War II. One may add that Pope John Paul II's passion for world peace cannot be truly grasped without some knowledge of World War II and his experiences during those years.

On September 1, 1939, without any declaration of war, the German warship *Schleswig-Holstein*, on a "courtesy visit" to Gdansk, opened fire on the Polish fort of Westerplatte. World War II had begun, and Poland, as one historian put it, entered its period of greatest trial, its Golgotha.

While the German air force bombed Polish cities, and tanks devastated the countryside, the Russians, claiming that Poland had "ceased to exist," crossed the eastern frontier and rapidly occupied half of the country. Only then did the rest of the world come to know that Germany and Russia had a secret agreement, the Ribbentrop-Molotov nonaggression pact, signed August 29, 1939, to carve up Poland between them. In conformity with the pact, Germany's slice of Poland covered 73,000 square miles (189,000 sq km) with 21.8 million people, while the Kremlin took 77,000 square miles (200,000 sq km) inhabited by 13.2 million people.

The Poles, in the eyes of the Nazis, were *untermenschen* (sub-human), and occupied a land that was part of the *lebenstraum* (living space) coveted by the German race. Before the German invasion of Poland, Hitler made it clear that the destruction of Poland was among the Third Reich's primary tasks. His command to the Nazi hierarchy: "The aim is. . . the annihilation of living forces. . . . Be merciless! Be brutal. . . . It is necessary to proceed with maximum severity. . . . The war is to be a war of annihilation." Heinrich Himmler, the man who implemented the German war on the Poles and other Slavs, echoed Hitler's will: "All Poles will disappear from the world . . . It is essential that the great German people should consider it a major task to destroy all Poles."

Hitler believed that if he was to realize his ambition of dominating Europe, he had to reduce Poland to a position of dependence or wipe it out altogether. Germany could not be free to dominate central Europe as long as Poland, considered a stubborn thorn in its side, existed on its eastern border.

As the Third Reich swiftly carried out plans for the cultural annihilation of Poland, it closed all scientific, artistic, and literary institutions. Polish history books were confiscated, monuments of Polish heroes were destroyed, and the names of Polish cities were Germanized. Within months, the Germans stripped major art collections and destroyed most of Poland's archives.

Since Polish nationalism was synonymous with Catholicism, it was clear to the Nazis that they also had to destroy the organization and leadership of the Polish Church in order to exterminate the Polish nation. More than 3,600 Polish priests—about one in four—were sent to concentration camps, along with 1,117 nuns and 730 other ecclesiastics. Five and a half years of Nazi occupation claimed the lives of 1,932 priests, 850 monks, and 289 nuns. In addition, many laymen were also put to death for their faith. In regions near Germany, U.S. intelligence reported, "Practically the whole Catholic clergy of Polish descent has been eliminated by death, imprisonment, and exile."

On the eastern front, though the Soviets did not engage in mass killings or indiscriminate shootings of innocent people, some half a million Poles were deported to forced labor camps under inhuman conditions. For weeks, those deported journeyed in packed and unheated trains across vast Russian territory. Thousands died before reaching their destination; more than 125,000 died later from exhaustion and starvation at the labor camps.

OPPOSITE: *Bombed church in Gdansk, Poland, during World War II. The Roman Catholic Church, through its 1,000-year history in Poland, has weathered numerous attacks. Of these, the Nazi invasion inflicted the greatest damage. The Church was both above politics and at the heart of it.*
ABOVE: *Warsaw in ruins after Nazi bombing during World War II.*

Poland suffered at least as many civilian and military casualties during World War II as Austria, Britain, Belgium, Canada, France, Greece, Holland, Italy, Japan, Romania, the United States, and Yugoslavia combined. Approximately six million Poles were killed during the war. In the Warsaw Uprising alone, as many Poles were killed in sixty-three days as Americans during the whole of World War II.

The Laborer

From a life of the mind at Jagiellonian University, Karol was forced during World War II into a life of hard labor. All Polish adults and Jews of twelve years of age and older were ordered to do compulsory labor for the German war effort. Preferring this to other less desirable fates, Karol entered the labor force and received the *ausweiss*, an identity card that protected him from capture and deportation.

A friend of Karol's had recommended him to Henryk Kulakowski, manager of the Belgian-owned Solvay chemical company. Located in Zakrzówek, on the outskirts of Kraków, Solvay had been taken over by the Germans to help support the war effort; its Polish manager was retained for his expertise. A member of the Polish underground resistance, Kulakowski used his position at Solvay to provide protection for various members of the Polish intelligentsia.

When Karol was hired by Kulakowski in autumn 1940, he was first assigned to lay tracks at the plant's quarry. Later he was given the task of breaking up large blocks of limestone with a pick ax and loading them into trolleys. For eight hours at a stretch, Karol worked in below-freezing temperatures, clad in a heavily soiled blue uniform and wooden clogs.

Despite the demands at Solvay, Karol managed to carry on his work with the underground Rhapsodic Theater. He took advantage of the long walks to and from work to rehearse his parts, reciting Polish classics through the fields.

Karol quickly grew thin from the hard labor. He worked amid men who were numbed with fatigue, smashing rock and setting off dynamite charges in the steep canyon. In the spring of 1941, a Solvay supervisor named Krause helped Karol get reassigned to an easier job at the quarry. An ethnic German, Krause had grown up among Poles and tried to improve the lot of the young intellectuals working at Solvay. Karol's new job had him placing the explosives that Wojciech Zukrowski, a friend from the Jagiellonian University, then ignited.

An underground resistance group was, by this time, rapidly growing in Poland. Zukrowski, who was a member of the group, took advantage of his position to steal explosives for the resistance. His apartment also served as a support base for Allied prisoners fleeing the Nazis. Aware that Karol was not in favor of violent resistance, Zukrowski refrained from asking him to join the underground movement.

OPPOSITE: *The pope wearing a hardhat in 1982. An ex-quarry worker, the pope takes much time to learn about the plight of laborers.*
RIGHT: *Cardinal Wojtyla receives a delegation of Polish miners at Krakow's royal castle, the Wawel Cathedral. He was a strong proponent of the worker-priest movement, through which priests were sent to docks and factories to share the workers' lives.*

Karol stood firm on his nonviolent stance, even after the Nazis arrested the Salesian fathers from his parish church and deported them to a concentration camp, where twelve of the priests, including their superior, eventually died.

During the summer of 1941, Karol was transferred to Solvay's bicarbonate plant in the town of Borek Falecki. Although the plant was a two-hour walk each way, this facility provided better working conditions. For three years, Karol carried buckets of whitewash from limestone calcination furnaces to be used in water purification. Once the required quantity of lime and other substances had been delivered, Karol found time to read religious texts in the boiler room. His coworkers, Karol later recalled after becoming pope, happily kept watch so that he could concentrate on his reading.

On February 29, 1944, while Karol was walking home from work, he was hit by a speeding German truck and thrown off the road. Karol lay bloody and unconscious as the truck's driver, heedless of the accident, sped off. Jozefa Florek, a resident in the area, flagged down a passing car. The German officer in the car had Karol taken to a nearby hospital.

For two weeks, Karol recuperated in the hospital from a severe concussion, bad bruises, and a shoulder injury. His head was bandaged and his arm was placed in a cast. His hospital stay, Karol said later, turned out to be "a spiritual retreat" that gave him the opportunity to pray and meditate, and be at peace with his decision to enter the priesthood.

ABOVE: *The pope waves to a huge crowd in Gdansk, Poland, on June 12, 1987. Afterward, a group of people marched into the city carrying banners in defiance of the ban imposed by communist authorities on the Solidarity Union. During the week of his third visit in Poland since becoming pope, John Paul II grew steadily bolder as he challenged the government to prove its assertions of reform and urged Poles to persist in the pursuit of liberty.*

THE LIVING ROSARY

In 1940, Jan Tyranowski, a mystic who made his living as a tailor, approached Karol to become part of the Living Rosary. Karol was one of fifteen young men asked by Tyranowski to embody the fifteen mysteries of the Holy Rosary and pledge "to love God and neighbor" in every aspect of their daily existence.

Since the Nazis had already begun closing down seminaries and forbidding religious activities, the Living Rosary had to be strictly clandestine. Once a week, Tyranowski met in his shop with each of the members of the Living Rosary. The master, as he was called, guided the theological study, spiritual exercises, and prayer life of the Living Rosary members, tutoring them in the thought and mystical practices of Saints Teresa of Avila and John of the Cross.

Karol's involvement in the Living Rosary, which lasted about a year, helped form a spiritual discipline that would remain with him throughout his priesthood and papacy. As the master's motto was to devote each moment to one's spiritual growth and to loving service, Karol lived a structured life of prayer, meditation, Mass, and the study of religious text, while he worked as a waiter in a restaurant owned by his mother's brother. Like the rest of the Living Rosary members, he kept a spiritual diary, which he'd read to Tyranowski during their meetings.

Recalling his involvement in the Living Rosary, Pope John Paul II spoke about Tyranowski as "one of those unknown saints . . . who represented a new world I did not yet know." Through Tyranowski's spirituality, he said, "I saw the beauty of the soul opened up by grace."

LEFT: *Sculpture of St. Teresa of Avila in ecstasy by Gianlorenzo Bernini (1598–1680) at the Church of Santa Maria della Vittoria, Cornaro Chapel, in Rome, Italy.*

The Secret Seminarian

Karol's call to the priesthood took years to come into focus. Recalling this time, the pope wrote, "In the face of the spread of evil and the atrocities of war, the meaning of the priesthood and its mission in the world became much clearer to me. . . . A light began to shine ever more brightly in the back of my mind—*the Lord wants me to become a priest. . . .*"

While Karol had no intention of pursuing a religious vocation during his teens, his life had, for many years, been steeped in a monastic rhythm of prayer. The deaths of his father and brother, and the horrors of World War II called Karol to an even deeper commitment to prayer and meditation. Karol sought God's guidance regarding his choice of vocation until a moment of

"great clarity" came to him. The pope recalls, "It was like an interior illumination which brought with it the joy and certainty of a new vocation. And this awareness filled me with great inner peace."

At first, Karol wanted to become a contemplative monk in the Carmelite order, but the Archbishop of Kraków, Adam Sapieha, declined his request for permission to enter the order. The archbishop explained that the Polish Church was in great need of priests as the death list of priests continued to grow. Karol wholeheartedly abided by the archbishop's wish. Archbishop Sapieha had a powerful influence on the formation of Karol's priesthood, and Karol saw in him the union of the mystical with the militant, of contemplation with action. Sapieha, said Karol, "awakened me for the priesthood."

In October 1942, while still working at the Solvay bicarbonate plant, Karol began his studies as an underground seminarian. He was well aware of the dangers of his vocation. By then, many underground seminarians, including some of his friends, had been arrested and executed by the Gestapo.

Being in Kraków, which was the center of German operations, the archbishop and other clergy in the city were not persecuted as much as their confreres in other areas of German-occupied Poland. Hitler sought to control the clergy in Kraków and gain their support to fight Soviet communism. Archbishop Sapieha, however, refused to cooperate with Hitler's forces, and played a key role in underground operations throughout the war.

On August 6, 1944, Hitler's forces drowned the Warsaw Uprising in blood and turned their attention to Kraków. Hitler had ordered his troops to smash any Polish resistance in the city. The SS and the gestapo combed the streets of Kraków, rounding up the men, house by house. Karol and his houseguests, the

OPPOSITE: *Maksymilian Kolbe (pictured), a Polish priest, volunteered to take the place of Franciszek Gajowniczek, a fellow Pole condemned to death at Auschwitz. For two weeks, Reverend Kolbe hung on to life without food and water, while praying aloud with his cell mates during every waking hour; he was finally killed with an injection of carbolic acid. Gajowniczek survived to attend his benefactor's beatification ceremony. Pope John Paul II canonized Reverend Kolbe in 1982.*

RIGHT: *The pope prays at the Death Wall (execution wall) during his visit to the Nazi concentration camp at Auschwitz on June 7, 1979. His meditations at Auschwitz wrestled with the problem of evil and honored those who risked and lost their lives for others.*

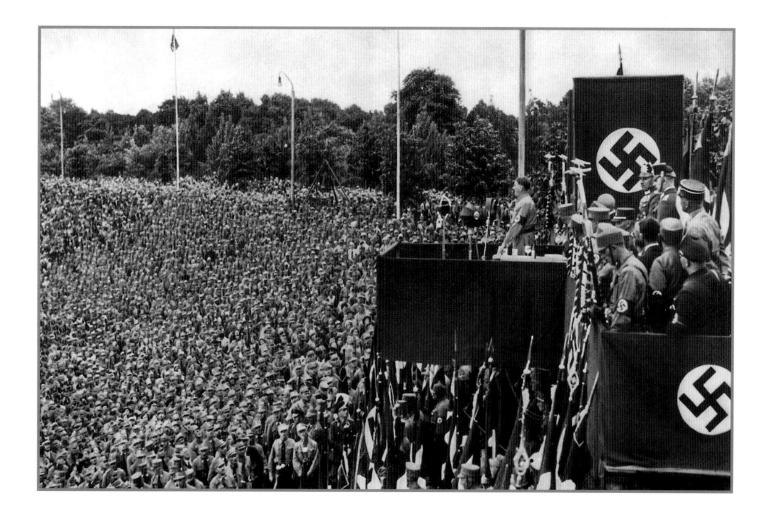

Kotlarczyks, were at home in the basement apartment of 10 Tyniecka Street when the German soldiers barged into the building. As they heard the shouts and pounding footsteps overhead, Karol knelt, then lay prostrate in fervent prayer, while the Kotlarczyks sat at the table, paralyzed in fear. After what seemed an eternity, the German soldiers left without stopping at the door leading to Karol's apartment. "I don't know how it happened," Mrs. Kotlarczyk recalled, "but the Germans didn't enter our quarters in the basement."

The following day, Archbishop Sapieha sent priests to fetch his remaining seminarians. From then on, they were to live and pursue their studies at the archbishop's residence, which would provide them with relative safety. Karol left his apartment and moved cautiously through empty streets. The previous day's massive roundup had left the city streets deserted. More than eight thousand men and boys had been taken away. Those left remained in their homes or in hiding. Karol approached the archbishop's palace under the eyes of a German sentinel overlooking a warehouse. By another stroke of luck, the guard ignored Karol, who reached his destination safely.

The seminarians undertook many months of training, until the end of the German occupation, without ever stepping out of the archbishop's residence. Meanwhile, because Karol remained in hiding, the Nazis began looking for him with urgent notices, followed by police visits at his apartment. Archbishop Sapieha sent Father Kazimierz Figlewicz to ask Solvay's manager, Kulakowski, to remove Karol's name from the workers' list. Kulakowski gladly complied with the request.

Contrary to Archbishop Sapieha's expectation, the Russians were in no hurry to advance into Kraków and liberate it from the Germans. The Red Army, on Stalin's orders, halted on the eastern side of the Vistula River and waited for the Germans to wipe out the Polish resistance fighters. On June 6, 1944 —D-day—Allied forces stormed the shores of northern France, striking a heavy blow against the Germans. By the summer of 1944, the Soviet army had "liberated" much of eastern Poland.

Although the war came to a close in 1945, Poland did not regain her independence. Some Polish communists, without any communication with the London-based Polish government-in-exile, announced that they had been recognized by Stalin as the new Polish government. The Yalta Conference of February 1945, through Stalin's maneuvering, resulted in the creation of a coalition government dominated by communists. The coalition assumed power on June 27, 1945, with a communist president and a communist premier.

When Jagiellonian University reopened, Karol returned to school and earned his degree in theology. On November 1, 1946,

OPPOSITE: *Adolf Hitler speaking in Dortmund, Germany, in 1933. Said an order from Hitler to Hans Frank, his governor general in Poland: "Priests will preach what we want them to preach . . . . The task of a priest is to keep the Poles quiet, stupid, and dull-witted." Wojtyla's vocation was a rebuttal of Hitler's will.*
ABOVE: *Alongside religious books, Karol Wojtyla studied the works of Marx, Lenin, and Stalin (pictured). He found conflict not between socialism and Church teachings, but between their methods of attaining justice.*

the feast of all saints, Archbishop Sapieha personally ordained Karol Wojtyla. The following day, Father Wojtyla celebrated his first three Masses at the crypt of Saint Leonard in the Wawel Cathedral. He chose to celebrate his first Masses in this cathedral (where the kings of Poland were buried) to express his spiritual bond with the history of Poland.

In the same month, Archbishop Sapieha sent Father Wojtyla to Rome for graduate studies at the Dominicans' Angelicum University. Following the advice of one of his superiors at the seminary in Kraków, Father Wojtyla made every effort to "learn Rome itself"—the Rome of the martyrs, the Rome of the catacombs, the Rome of Peter and Paul, and the Rome of the confessors of faith. "In Rome," wrote Pope John Paul II, "the early years of my priesthood had taken on both a European and a universal dimension."

After completing his studies in 1948, Father Wojtyla returned immediately to Poland. Although he graduated magna cum laude, he did not receive his doctorate for another thirty years, for he could not afford to pay for the publication of his dissertation, which he had titled *The Questions of Faith in the Works of Saint John of the Cross*. "As I left Rome," he recalled, "I took with me not only a much broader theological education, but also a strengthened priesthood and a more profound vision of the Church."

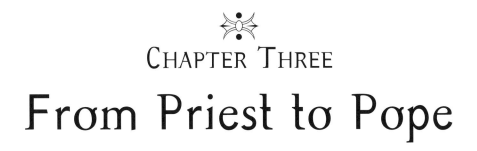

CHAPTER THREE

From Priest to Pope

The Priest

pon his return to Kraków from Rome, Father Wojtyla received his first "assignment" as priest. It was harvest time, late autumn in 1948, when Father Wojtyla, then twenty-eight years old, set out for his new parish in Niegowice, thirty miles (48km) from Kraków. He traveled by bus, cart, and finally, on foot. When he arrived in Niegowice, he knelt down amidst the fields of grain and kissed the ground. It was a gesture inspired by Saint Jean-Marie Vianney, whose priestly life and selfless service to his parish had inspired a spiritual revolution in nineteenth-century France.

At Niegowice, Father Wojtyla took charge of religious education in five elementary schools in the villages, celebrated Mass, heard confession, married couples, baptized babies, called on the sick, visited families, and blessed people's homes. He also took time to help villagers in various types of work, digging ditches and threshing wheat.

Father Wojtyla paid special attention to the youth, who called him *Wujek*, or uncle. He helped them in their studies, organized them into theatrical performances, and took them on cultural trips

to Kraków. The "eternal teenager," as some of his parishioners referred to him, Father Wojtyla seemed to relive his teenage years whenever he was with young people. He often played soccer and volleyball with his students. Around bonfires in the evenings, he sang and communed with them in prayer.

Communist authorities kept close watch on Father Wojtyla's activities. One of Wojtyla's young parishioners, Stanislaw Wyporek, was interrogated and beaten up by communist agents on false charges of belonging to a clandestine youth group. While comforting Stanislaw after the beating, Father Wojtyla advised

PAGE 36: *An undated portrait of Cardinal Wojtyla.*
PAGE 37: **Saint Peter in Tears.** *Guido Reni,*
c. 1575–1642. Palazzo Pitti, Florence.
OPPOSITE, LEFT: *Karol Wojtyla (center) with other*
young priests. Wojtyla's training for the priesthood
was in keeping with his vision of a Christian culture
that cultivated the wholeness in man: body, mind,
heart, feelings, and spirit.
OPPOSITE, RIGHT: *The young Father Wojtyla is*
remembered by peers as being charismatic, honest,
and possessed of a strong sense of self.
RIGHT: *Father Wojtyla was at once an intensely*
contemplative and an outgoing pastor.

him to tell the agents all the activities of the Catholic youth group as it had nothing to hide. "He never told us to resist," said Wyporek. "The bad things, he said, should be overcome by goodness, and that we should show our humility."

After a year of service in Niegowice, Father Wojtyla was transferred to St. Florian's Parish in Kraków. Archbishop Sapieha, then in his autumn years, was eager for Wojtyla to gain the experience of pastoring in both rural and urban settings.

At St. Florian's, Father Wojtyla taught catechism to senior high school students and provided pastoral care to university students. He became profoundly aware that addressing problems regarding love, sex, and marriage was an important part of the pastoral care of the youth. Through hearing confession and casual sharing, Father Wojtyla learned much about these matters and

reflected upon them deeply. Years later, he wrote *The Jeweler's Shop*, a play about the troubles of married couples, and the book *Love and Responsibility*. Both were published in 1960, when Wojtyla was already an auxiliary bishop.

After the death of Archbishop Sapieha in 1951, his successor, Eugeniusz Baziak, directed Father Wojtyla toward scholarly work that would qualify him to teach ethics and moral theology. Father Wojtyla studied the works of Martin Buber, Gabriel Marcel, Emmanuel Mounier, and above all, Max Scheler. The notion of love was central in Scheler's work. It is, as Scheler wrote, ". . . the pioneer of values, that is to say, by which the goodness of other values are discerned and discovered. Unless we love, we cannot know." Scheler believed that human nature was beyond scientific scrutiny, and that scientific objectivity itself depended on one's understanding of oneself and one's relation to the world.

Father Wojtyla's thesis on the work of Scheler, "Building a System of Christian Ethics on the Basis of Max Scheler's Philosophy," earned him his second doctorate from Jagiellonian University. Thereafter, he became part of the faculty of the Jagiellonian's department of theology, where he lectured on Christian ethics.

Father Wojtyla's teaching stint at the Jagiellonian was cut short when communist authorities closed down the university's theology department in 1954. In an effort to thwart Church operations, the authorities had imposed a ban on all Catholic organizations and refused to allow ration of newsprint to any Catholic publications.

The communist authorities were bent upon systematically destroying the Church in Poland. By the end of 1953, eight bishops and more than nine hundred priests, among them Archbishop Baziak and Cardinal Stefan Wyszyński, were in prison. Many of those imprisoned were known as or suspected of being a part of the resistance or were viewed as politically antagonistic to the communist cause.

Since Father Wojtyla's focus was pastoring and teaching, he gave the authorities no reason to arrest him. An academic colleague, historian Stefan Swiezawski, recalls that Wojtyla's attitude was to use each moment to strengthen his orientation and to expand his knowledge rather than engage himself in politics.

In 1956 Wojtyla was appointed director of the ethics department at the Catholic University of Lublin, the only university run by the Catholic Church in the vast territory under the dominion of Stalin's heirs and Mao Tse-tung.

After the death of Stalin in 1953, unrest continued to spread in Poland, erupting in Poznan, an industrial town 175 miles (280km) west of Warsaw. Tens of thousands of Polish demonstrators took to the streets in June 1956, demanding better working conditions and pay raises. Demonstrators tore down Soviet flags, besieged party headquarters, overturned state cars, and set fire to a prison. More than two hundred people, including some police, died, and many more were injured.

Two months later, in August, one and a half million Poles gathered in Częstochowa for the annual pilgrimage in honor of the Black Madonna and the three hundredth anniversary of the victory of the Polish army against the invading Swedes. Together, the pilgrims prayed the Great Novena and read King Kazimierz's message to Mary. "Queen of Poland! Today we renew the vows of our ancestors," the message began. The faithful proceeded by reciting a list of vows—which requested, essentially, that Poles keep their faith and surrender their lives to divine will. To each pledge, a million and a half voices vowed in unison: "Queen of Poland, we promise!"

OPPOSITE: *Karol Wojtyla hiking in 1953. He enjoyed abundant vacations, hiking, skiing, and kayaking. In 1954, he won an award from the Polish Tourist Society for the number of miles he had hiked. In 1955, he entered an international kayaking competition in which he ripped the hull of his boat on some rocks.*
ABOVE: *The pope skiing in 1984. Some of Wojtyla's friends referred to him as a "daredevil skier."*

In October, while Father Wojtyla was on an extended bicycle trip with his students, an anti-Stalin reformist faction of the Polish communist party came to power. Led by Wladyslaw Gomulka, the party released many of Poland's political prisoners, including Cardinal Wyszyński. As Soviet forces advanced west of Warsaw, Gomulka warned Soviet secretary Nikita Khrushchev that the Poles would fight. On October 20, Khrushchev caved in, recognizing Gomulka as the new Polish leader, but he installed a contingent of pro-Moscow men on the Central Committee to watch him.

ABOVE: *Wladyslaw Gomulka speaks at a harvest festival in Warsaw, before his visit to Belgrade in November 1957. Through Gomulka's initiative, many of Poland's prisoners, including Cardinal Stefan Wyszyński, were released.*

ON LOVE AND RESPONSIBILITY

Stirred by the sanctity of the love between husband and wife, of which sex is so much a part, Karol Wojtyla, as priest and bishop, wrote extensively about the subject of romantic love. Owing to the depth and openness with which Wojtyla has tackled the subject, his writings on human love have had a significant impact on Church teachings in the field of moral problems related to sex and family.

Wojtyla's book *Love and Responsibility* (1960) stirred much controversy due to its unabashed discussion of sexual matters. Many, however, consider it to be a literary tour de force on sexuality from the perspective of Christian ethics. Within its chapters, Wojtyla deals with the concept of virginity, sexual psychopathology, the religious dimension of sexual drive, and the metaphysics of love. *Love and Responsibility* became a bestseller, with hundreds of thousands of copies sold in Poland. It has been translated into many languages, including English, French, Spanish, Italian, German, Portuguese, Swedish, and Japanese.

Wojtyla's play on marriage as spiritual path, *The Jeweler's Shop*, was also published in 1960. The play is a meditation on the spiritual dimension of married life. Many of Wojtyla's conversations with his young students found their way into this work, in which Wojtyla's characters delve deeply into the mysteries of human love. The character of Adam, the mysterious stranger who has never been married and acts as witness and adviser to the couples in the play, states these lines:

The divergence between what lies on the surface and the mystery of love constitutes precisely the source of drama. It is one of the greatest dramas of human existence. The surface of love has its current—swift, flickering, changeable. . . . The current is sometimes so stunning that it carries people away—men and women. They get carried away by the thought that they have absorbed the whole secret of love, but in fact they have not even touched it. They are happy for a while, thinking they have reached the limits of existence and wrested all its secrets from it so that nothing remains. . . . But there can't be nothing: there can't! . . . Man is a continuum, a totality and a continuity—so it cannot be that nothing remains!

—FROM *THE JEWELER'S SHOP*

LEFT: *Wojtyla's writings on love, marriage, and sex provide a unified view of sense and spirit.*

The Road to Rome

In July 1958, Cardinal Stefan Wyszyński received a telegram from the Holy Father appointing Karol Josef Wojtyla, at age thirty-eight, auxiliary bishop of Kraków. It was the first time the cardinal, a staunch conservative, had been bypassed in the appointment of a Polish bishop. Since communist authorities made it difficult to conduct Church business, Pope Pius XII had granted Cardinal Wyszyński the privilege of selecting potential bishops. The cardinal kept on hand a list of candidates for approval by the pope. The list did not include Wojtyla's name.

Father Wojtyla was on vacation at the Mazurian Lakes when he was summoned by Cardinal Wyszyński. The cardinal read to him the pope's letter: "At the request of Archbishop Baziak, I am appointing Father Karol Wojtyla auxiliary bishop of Kraków; kindly express your approval of this appointment."

Wojtyla did not hesitate to accept the appointment. After leaving the cardinal's palace, he rushed to the convent of the Grey Ursuline Sisters on the bank of the Vistula River, where he knew

he could find the silence he needed in order to pray. According to the nuns who saw him in the chapel, Wojtyla remained immersed in prayer and meditation for no less than eight hours.

On September 28, 1958, Karol Wojtyla was consecrated bishop in the Wawel Cathedral in Kraków. He had the letter *M* (for Mary, the Mother of God) and the words *Totus Tuus* ("I'm all yours") inscribed on his coat of arms. His new appointment didn't alter his lifestyle. Despite suggestions from his superiors and staff to move to a well-appointed church facility and to upgrade his manner of dressing, he continued to live in his small two-bedroom apartment and wear his patched, threadbare cassocks and worn-out shoes. Instead of riding in a car, he insisted on biking his way around.

On October 9, 1958, Pope Pius XII died at the age of eighty-two. Before the end of October, Angelo Giuseppe Roncalli, seventy-seven, became Pope John XXIII. The new pope, desiring to make the greatest contribution to the Church during the remaining years of his life, lost no time in calling for a Church Council, the first in ninety years. Soon the new bishop of Kraków would join over 2,300 bishops from around the world in the revolution that was to be the Second Vatican Council (1962–1965).

On December 30, 1963, Bishop Karol Wojtyla, forty-three, was appointed Metropolitan Archbishop of Kraków by the pope. The communist regime, which had a hand in Wojtyla's appointment, had no inkling that their man of choice would, in the future, play a key role in the dismantling of communist rule in Europe.

Tad Szulc writes on this historical irony in *Pope John Paul II: The Biography*, "The truth concerning these events is extremely important because it establishes beyond doubt that the communist regime in Warsaw, wholly misunderstanding the realities of the Polish church and its personalities, was directly responsible for

OPPOSITE: *The 600-year-old Wawel Cathedral in Kraków is where Wojtyla's ordination and the ceremonies for his elevation to bishop, archbishop, and cardinal took place. Polish kings lived in the Wawel Castle adjoining the cathedral until the seventeenth century and were buried in the cathedral's basement.*

ABOVE: *Cardinal Stefan Wyszyński, primate of Poland, and Cardinal Wojtyla. Although they had serious differences, Wojtyla managed to overlook them in favor of preserving their unity.*

From Priest to Pope

Wojtyla's appointment as archbishop. This, in turn, led to his cardinalcy and his eventual elevation to the pontificate. The ultimate historical irony was, of course, the decisive role played by John Paul II in the negotiations resulting in the demise of communist rule first in Poland and subsequently elsewhere."

Cardinal Wyszyński had submitted six names to the communist authorities for the post of archbishop. The six, which did not include Wojtyla, were rejected in succession. Wyszyński finally proposed Wojtyla. Stanislaw Stomma, the official intermediary between the episcopate and the regime, recounts that he was consulted by Zenon Kliszko, the number-two man in the Polish communist establishment, as to who would be the best candidate for archbishop of Kraków. Stomma told Kliszko that Wojtyla would be "the best and only choice" for the regime, should it insist that only bishops who were apolitical and who would stick to pastoral work be approved for promotion. The committee went by Stomma's advice, approving Wojtyla's appointment.

The communist authorities were caught in an unpleasant surprise, as Wojtyla turned out to be a tough-minded archbishop. He drowned the authorities with ceaseless requests for permission to build more churches and seminaries; requests for permits for processions and pilgrimages; and complaints over the

OPPOSITE: *From the ramparts of the Wawel Cathedral in Krakow, Karol Wojtyla is elevated to cardinal in July 1967.*
ABOVE: *As a new leader of the Roman Catholic Church, Cardinal Wojtyla takes time out to feed the native animals during his trip to Australia to attend the 1973 Eucharistic Congress.*

drafting of seminarians for military service. He generously supported intellectual groups that were part of the cultural resistance and spoke openly against the regime when students were beaten up at rallies.

Despite his outspoken stance toward the communist regime, Wojtyla, observers noted, remained nonconfrontational. As Carl Bernstein and Marco Politi noted in *His Holiness*, Wojtyla's confrontation with communism took place not in the context of a specific religious denomination or ideological issue, but in regard to the rights of human beings, pure and simple. Jerzy Turowicz, editor of the *Catholic Weekly* in Kraków, wrote: "He is not a leftist, he's not a rightist, and he's not a nationalist either."

Archbishop Wojtyla set up a family institute to help families deal with domestic problems and formed a ministry to look after the sick and the disabled. He gathered professionals from all over the country to collaborate in finding solutions to problems they were facing in their practice. He also organized ongoing multidisciplinary symposia for the advancement of knowledge in various fields of study.

Pope John XXIII died on June 3, 1963, six months after issuing his *Pacem in Terris* (Peace on Earth) encyclical, the first significant step taken by the Vatican to help in the long effort to bring an end to the Cold War. Pope John had insisted on ongoing dialogue with the communist world. While Premier Khrushchev and President Kennedy negotiated on limiting certain kinds of weaponry, *Pacem in Terris* urged an outright ban on nuclear weapons.

Cardinal Giovanni Battista Montini was elected pope on June 21, 1963, taking on the name Paul VI. The new pope would pursue his predecessor's work in building bridges to the communist east. In 1967 Paul VI made Wojtyla, at the age of forty-seven, a cardinal, and began to groom the young cardinal for greater tasks. Wojtyla was named to various Vatican committees—Clergy, Catholic Education, Liturgy, and Oriental Churches; and was appointed consultor to the Council of Laity.

In 1976 Paul VI asked Cardinal Wojtyla to deliver the Lenten spiritual exercises for members of the Curia and the papal household. Cardinal Wojtyla's meditations on the transforming power of love deeply moved Paul VI, who at various occasions had spoken of the creation of a civilization of love.

Cardinal Wojtyla's most impassioned declarations on human rights were delivered before thousands of young students during the Corpus Christi processions of 1977 and 1978. He said, "Human rights cannot be given in the form of concessions. Man is born with them and seeks to realize them in the course of his life. And if they are not realized or experienced, then man rebels. And it cannot be otherwise, because he is man. His sense of honor expects it."

On August 7, 1978, Paul VI died from a massive heart attack. His successor, Pope John Paul I, died on September 28, 1978, after only thirty-four days in office. On October 3, Primate Wyszyński and Cardinal Wojtyla flew to Rome to participate in the conclave to choose the next pope.

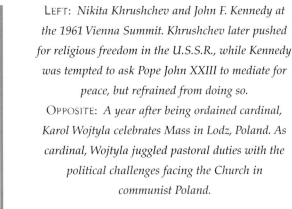

LEFT: *Nikita Khrushchev and John F. Kennedy at the 1961 Vienna Summit. Khrushchev later pushed for religious freedom in the U.S.S.R., while Kennedy was tempted to ask Pope John XXIII to mediate for peace, but refrained from doing so.*
OPPOSITE: *A year after being ordained cardinal, Karol Wojtyla celebrates Mass in Lodz, Poland. As cardinal, Wojtyla juggled pastoral duties with the political challenges facing the Church in communist Poland.*

Church Renewal

Less than three months after he became pope, John XXIII felt a great need "to open the windows of the Church and let the fresh air in." Without hesitation, he summoned the Second Vatican Council, an action that would alter almost every aspect of the life of the Roman Catholic Church.

This council, in session between October and December of each year from 1962 through 1965, gathered 2,381 bishops, superiors of religious orders, and cardinals to reexamine every aspect of the Roman Catholic faith. One of those invited was Kraków's bishop, Karol Josef Wojtyla.

In summoning the council, Pope John XXIII called for *aggiornamento*, a renewal. A genuine renewal, he believed, could come about only if the leadership of the Church would allow itself to be led by the Spirit in order that it may truly lead. On the evening of the council's opening, John XXIII joked, "We are all novices. The Holy Spirit will certainly be present when the bishops gather, and we'll see what happens."

Vatican II was unlike any of the twenty councils preceding it, from Nicea in 325 to the First Vatican Council in 1869. In style and content, it reflected a significant shift from being reactionary to being responsive to the challenges facing the Church. "It was not a defensive style. . . . It was characterized by great openness to dialogue," wrote Pope John Paul II in *Crossing the Threshold of Hope*. He recounts his recollections of the spirit of dialogue:

The dialogue was not intended to be limited to Christians alone. It was meant to be open to non-Christian religions, and to reach the whole modern world. . . . *Truth, in fact, cannot be confined.* Truth is for one and for all. And if this truth comes about through love (cf. Eph. 4:15), then it becomes even more universal. This was the style of the Second Vatican Council and the spirit in which it took place.

This style and this spirit will be remembered as the essential truth about the Council, not the controversies between "liberals" and "conservatives"— controversies seen in political, not religious, terms—to which some people wanted to reduce the whole Council. In this spirit the Second Vatican Council will continue to be a challenge for all churches and a duty for each person for a long time to come.

In the council's spirit, John Paul II has made unprecedented strides in ecumenical dialogue, rapprochements with Protestant and Eastern Orthodox communities, openings to other religions, dialogue with nonbelievers, the disavowal of anti-Semitism, and above all, the reorientation of power from the Church hierarchy to the laity.

Pope John XXIII in 1960. By calling Vatican Council II, he forced the church to redefine its meaning for the world. The architect of this council left a legacy that would renew the Church from within.

Patrick Keegan, a prominent member of various international lay organizations, credits Bishop Wojtyla as one of the primary architects of *Lumen Gentium*, the document that moved away from the idea of the Church as a monarchical pyramid, toward a new concept of the Church as a body in which everyone is responsible for its mission, but each in his or her own way. "As one of those responsible for this crucial document, Wojtyla knows that this change of emphasis is one of the most important things that happened in the Council," said Keegan. "Because of it, the Church moved on to a new track."

Additionally, it was Wojtyla who impressed upon the council that atheists had to be understood, not preached to. When the council was discussing the problems of atheism—a question that had vexed the Council Fathers from the very beginning—Wojtyla declared, when he took the floor on October 21, 1964: "It is not the Church's role to lecture unbelievers. We are involved in a quest along with our fellow men. . . . Let us avoid all moralizing and all suggestion that we have a monopoly on the truth." He then suggested for the Church to take the heuristic approach in education, which "allows the pupil to go find the truth, as it were, on his own."

At the height of the debate on religious freedom, Wojtyla's input altered the trend of the discussion, which had been dominated by authoritarian conservatives. Himself a conservative, yet open-minded and ready for debate, Wojtyla cried, "Do not hesitate to call for religious freedom. Such an affirmation would be of capital importance for those of us who live under communist regimes."

In closing the Second Vatican Council, on December 8, 1965, Pope Paul VI, carrying on the work of the council after the death of John XXIII, exclaimed, "No one in the world is a stranger, no one is excluded, no one is far away."

As pope, Wojtyla would see himself as the implementor of Vatican II. He draws a clear line between the Church of the past and that of the present. "We find ourselves faced with a new reality. *The world, tired of ideology, is opening itself to truth*," he wrote in *Crossing the Threshold of Hope*. "The time has come when the splendor of this truth (*veritatis splendor*) has begun anew to illuminate the darkness of human existence. Even if it is too early to judge, if we consider how much has been accomplished, it is clear that *the Council will not remain a dead letter*."

Chapter Four
The Pilgrim Pope

The Conclave: *Habemus Papam!*

As the conclave to choose the successor to Pope John Paul I began, only a few had any notion that Karol Wojtyla would become the next pope. But as Cardinal Enrique y Tarancon later summed up what had happened during the election, "God forced us to break with history to elect Karol Wojtyla."

Only two months after Albino Luciani had been elected Pope John Paul I, a hundred and eleven cardinals from around the world were called back to Rome. The responsibility of choosing the man who would lead the universal Church of nearly one billion faithful at a critical point in the Church's history weighed heavily upon the shoulders of the cardinals. A majority vote of two-thirds plus one was needed to elect the new pope, Peter's 263rd successor.

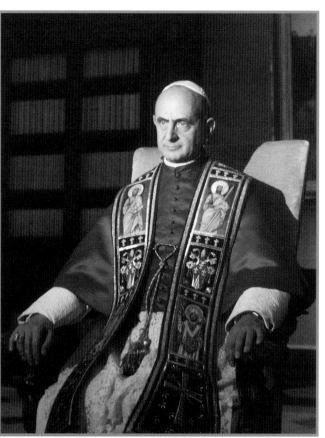

After just thirty-four days in office, Pope John Paul I died of a heart attack. Those close to him said that Albino Luciani essentially broke down from the heavy burden of responsibility, stress, and isolation. From the moment he was elected pope, Luciani had shown signs of distress. When Belgian Cardinal Leo Joseph Suenens embraced and thanked the newly elected pope for saying yes to his election, the latter replied, "Perhaps it would have been better if I said no." Vatican secretary of state Jean Villot recounts that Pope John Paul I had told him a few days before his death, "Another man better than I could have

been chosen. Paul VI already pointed out his successor: He was sitting just in front of me in the Sistine Chapel. . . . He will come, because I will go." The man to whom he was referring was Cardinal Wojtyla.

Most of the cardinals, however, had not decided on their choice or did not have Cardinal Wojtyla in mind when the conclave began. On the first day of balloting, October 15, 1978, it was mainly a contest between Cardinal Guiseppe Siri, the arch conservative of the lot, and Cardinal Giovanni Benelli, a strong advocate of Vatican II reforms. Both, however, failed to get a majority vote by the end of the day.

The deadlock gave rise to much uncertainty among the cardinals, who were still predisposed to elect an Italian. There were, of course, many outstanding non-Italians, but none of them had come into focus. Years later, Cardinal Koenig described to *Time* magazine's Vatican correspondent Wilton Wynn the mood of uncertainty that evening: "We dined together but there was very little discussion, no lobbying. In the fresh air of the courtyard of San Damaso, we took our walks silently. We felt a strange tension in our minds. There was no human explanation for the choice that we made the next day."

During the idle moments of the conclave, Cardinal Wojtyla was seen with his nose buried in a Marxist journal, seemingly unperturbed by the gravity of the task at hand. The second day,

PAGE 52: *The newly-elected Pope John Paul II.*

PAGE 53: *Statue of St. Peter at St. Peter's Basilica.*

OPPOSITE: *Pope Paul VI (pictured), who carried on Pope John XXIII's* **Ostpolitik** *opening to the East, paved the way for John Paul II's role in the opening of Eastern Europe.*

ABOVE: *Cardinals file into the Sistine Chapel on October 14, 1978 to elect Pope John Paul I's successor. The pre-conclave politicking gives way to absolute silence.*

ABOVE: *The pope kisses thirteen-month-old Jennifer Pearce during a service for the sick and disabled at Southwark Cathedral, England, 1982. Children get a special dose of papal attention.*

OPPOSITE: *Pope John Paul I, the pope with a beaming smile, had neither curial nor international experience. A curial official said his death "could have had something to do with going from bearing responsibility for a relatively small diocese of 600,000 Catholics in Venice to taking on the responsibility for the entire Catholic world." The "smiling pope" would have rather lived a simple life.*

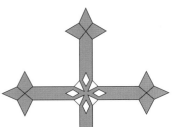

however, tested Cardinal Wojtyla's composure. His name, which had not been heard before in the conclave, was read by the *scrutatore* on a few ballots. Wojtyla's supporters, Cardinal Franz Koenig from Vienna and Cardinal John Krol from Philadelphia, had patiently spread word of his merits and floated the idea that it was time to vote for a non-Italian pope.

When Cardinal Wojtyla's name was pronounced, as Wynn wrote, "it was as if the dove had landed on [his] head." A majority began to form in his favor. During a break, Cardinal Wojtyla was glimpsed in the cell of Primate Wyszyński, weeping and collapsing in the primate's arms. The Polish primate, whose rigid conservatism had hitherto kept Wojtyla at arm's length, said, "If they elect you, you must accept. For Poland."

Two ballots later, Wojtyla's name was announced. Ninety-four cardinals had given him their vote. Wojtyla accepted his election with a solemn, albeit untraditional vow. Instead of simply saying yes, as tradition dictated, the new pope said, in his incisive baritone voice, "With obedience in faith to Christ, my Lord, and with trust in the Mother of Christ and of the Church, in spite of the great difficulties, I accept." The cardinals broke out in applause. Wojtyla took the name John Paul II.

After his acceptance, Wojtyla was escorted to the scarlet-walled crying room, the *camera lacrimatoria*. In the back of the Sistine Chapel, the stove spewed out white smoke to announce to the world that a pope had been chosen.

ABOVE: *The morning after his election to the papacy, Pope John Paul II celebrates Mass with all the cardinals.*

ABOVE: *Cardinals pay their respects to the newly elected pope on the steps of St. Peter's Basilica.*

ABOVE: *At his first* **Urbi et Orbi** *(City and the World) blessing, the pope endears himself to the mostly Roman audience by speaking Italian, one of many languages Wojtyla has taught himself.*

OPPOSITE, TOP: *Cardinals file in front of St. Peter's Basilica during consecration rites for Pope John Paul II.*

OPPOSITE, BOTTOM: *A huge crowd awaits the announcement of the new pope at St. Peter's Square.*

A break with history had occurred—the first non-Italian Pope in 256 years; the youngest since Pio Nono, elected in 1864 at age forty-four; the first from behind the Iron Curtain, a country with a Marxist and atheist government.

Returning to the Sistine Chapel, John Paul II was led to an armchair placed in front of the altar where, as tradition would have it, he was to sit and receive the obeisance of the cardinals. When he was invited to sit, the pope replied, "No, I receive my brothers standing up." Thereupon, he warmly embraced each of the cardinals.

More than two hundred thousand faithful stood waiting at the square of St. Peter's Basilica for the new pope to be introduced. At sundown, Cardinal Felici stepped out of the balcony facing the

square. He declared in Latin, "I announce to you in great joy. . . . We have a pope!—*Habemus Papam*!" When the roar of the crowd died down, Cardinal Felici announced the new pope's name. A moment of silence swept across St. Peter's Square as the multilingual crowd wondered where the new pope was from. With an African-sounding name, the new pope was thought by many to be African. Then someone cried out: "He's Polish!"

With a smile on his face, John Paul II stepped forward to bestow his first *Urbi et Orbi* (City and the World) blessing. He delivered a brief address in Italian: "May Jesus Christ be praised! . . . I do not know whether I can explain myself well in your— our—Italian language. If I make a mistake, you will correct me.

Meanwhile, Polish communist authorities began dealing with the repercussions of Wojtyla's election. A communist journalist gave Stewart Steven, author of *The Poles*, this reaction upon learning of Wojtyla's election: "I was out of the country attending an international seminar in Prague, and a Czech, knowing I was Polish, came up to me and told me the news. My first thought was, 'This means trouble.' My second thought was, 'This means very big trouble.'"

And so I present myself to you all to confess our common faith, our hope, our confidence in the Mother of Christ and of the Church, and also to start anew on this road of history and of the Church, with the help of God. . . ."

John Paul II's first days in office were a preview of things to come: a defiance of rigid protocol, a preference for doing things his way, and a passion for dialogue with those of other faiths. Wearing a plain black cassock, he left the Vatican palace with only two bodyguards to visit an ailing friend, Bishop Deskur, at the hospital. He received childhood friends and their families at an informal ceremony called "Farewell to the Motherland." His first press conference treated two thousand journalists to a casualness and a freedom of speech not experienced with other popes. He met with heads of non–Roman Catholic churches, holding hands with them in a circle of prayer for unity and cooperation.

OPPOSITE, LEFT: *John Paul II celebrating Mass with the Black Madonna in the background.*

OPPOSITE, RIGHT: *The pope delivers many of his messages from a window of the Vatican apartments.*

ABOVE: *John Paul II celebrates Mass during his first visit to Poland as pope in 1979, drawing millions of people. None of the anticipated problems came about—the behavior both of the crowds and the communist forces was exemplary.*

ABOVE: *The pope waves to the crowd while riding down Broadway in New York City on October 3, 1979.*
Holding the umbrella is New York Cardinal Terence Cooke.

ABOVE: *Pope John Paul II waves to a cheering crowd at Shea Stadium in New York on October 3, 1979. In one of his speeches in New York, the pope said: "We must find a simple way of living. . . . It is not right that the standard of living of rich countries should . . . maintain itself by drawing off . . . the reserves of energy and raw materials that are meant to serve the whole of humanity."*

Mother Saves the Day

On the afternoon of May 13, 1981, as the popemobile was inching its way through the open-air papal audience at St. Peter's square, Mehmet Ali Agca, an experienced assassin, fired two shots at Pope John Paul II from within a twenty-foot (6.1m) range.

At the precise moment that Agca fired the shots, the pope bent down to hug a young girl who was wearing a small likeness of the image of Our Lady of Fatima. The bullets missed the pope but hit two pilgrims standing nearby. Had the pope not bent down to hug the eighteen-month-old girl, the bullets would have ripped through his skull.

Agca fired again, hitting the pope in the abdomen. The pope fell on the lap of his chamberlain. On the way to the hospital, the pope, in agony, repeatedly whispered in Polish, "Mary, my mother . . . Mary, my mother."

The pope lost consciousness when he reached the hospital. His blood pressure was falling; his pulse nearly silenced. By the time the head surgeon, Dr. Francesco Crucitti, cut open his abdomen, the pope had lost three-fourths of his blood from internal hemorrhaging. The 9mm bullet from the Browning Parabellum pistol shattered his colon and small intestine, and passed through the sacral system.

A massive blood transfusion was performed. Twenty-two inches (56cm) of the pope's intestines had to be cut away, the colon lacerations sewn up, and injuries to his right shoulder and a finger on his left hand (caused when the bullet exited his body)

treated during the five-and-a-half-hour operation. An opening on the colon, a colostomy, was made for temporary drainage.

The attending surgeons considered the projectile's trajectory "miraculous"—John Paul II would have died instantly had the bullet not missed the central aorta by a few millimeters.

Five days after the assassination attempt, on his sixty-first birthday, the pope started working from his hospital room, against the advice of his doctors. He celebrated Mass, held meetings, checked the galleys of his next encyclical, and taped messages to the faithful. The pope said in one of his messages, "I am praying for the brother who wounded me and whom I sincerely forgive."

John Paul II had known that he was courting danger. Five days after the Vatican announced the pope's scheduled meeting with the Orthodox Patriarch Dimitrios I in Istanbul at the end of November 1979, the twenty-one-year-old Mehmet Ali Agca escaped from prison. He was smuggled out of prison by friends from the Gray Wolves, a neo-Nazi terrorist organization that has menaced Turks since the 1960s. Agca had admitted to the murder of a prominent Istanbul newspaper editor who was a strong advocate of modern reforms in the Islamic community.

After Agca's escape, the murdered editor's newspaper received and published a letter from Agca, stating, "Western imperialism has . . . dispatched to Turkey in the guise of a religious leader the Crusade commander John Paul. Unless this timely and meaningless visit is postponed, I shall certainly shoot the pope."

In January of 1980, Alexandre de Marenches, head of the French secret service, sent an emissary to the Vatican to warn the pope of a communist plot on his life. In February of 1981, an hour before the pope was to visit the municipal stadium in Karachi, a bomb exploded, killing the man who was carrying it. Such warnings did not curb the pontiff's schedule of public appearances. The French intelligence chief later wrote in his memoirs, "The Holy Father replied that his destiny was in the hands of God."

The pope became convinced that divine intervention, through the Lady of Fatima, had saved his life. The shooting occurred on the feast day of the Lady, who is believed to have appeared to three Portuguese children in 1917 in a series of six apparitions. The pope was shot at 5:19PM, the exact time of day he was elected pope on October 16, 1978.

OPPOSITE: *The pope's love of babies helped save his life during the assassination attempt.*
RIGHT: *Aides hold the pope after Agca's bullet hit him. John Paul II stayed awake, praying aloud during the four-mile (6.4km) trip to the Gamelli Clinic.*

RIGHT: *John Paul II in a popemobile on a visit to the United States. After the attempt on his life, the pope, much to his dismay, was persuaded to move around in a bullet-proof glass enclosure.*

OPPOSITE, LEFT: *The pope sits in deep thought. He did not surrender control of the Vatican establishment during the long weeks of convalescence after the assassination attempt. Through eighteen years of investigation about who was behind the attempt on his life, the pope has remained quiet on the issue.*

OPPOSITE, RIGHT: *The pope visits Mehmet Ali Agca in his cell at Rome's Rebibbia prison. He took Agca's hand in his several times as they conversed, sitting on chairs facing each other. The pope has regularly had parcels of Turkish delicacies sent to Agca in his prison cell.*

The Pilgrim Pope

In prison, Agca was said to have developed an obsession and a fear of the Lady after learning that the pope had come to believe that the Lady had saved his life. "One hand fired," said the pope, "and another guided the bullet."

When the pope paid Agca a visit in his prison cell in December of 1983, he embraced his assassin who, in turn, kissed the pontiff's hand. For about twenty minutes, the two spoke in private, often whispering into each other's ears. While most of the contents of the conversation have remained private, Agca told reporters that he begged the pope to tell him about the "mystery" of Fatima. He also was reported to have asked the pope: "Tell me, why it is that I could not kill you?"

The truth behind the attempt on the pontiff's life, in the words of former CIA director Robert Gates, is "the last great secret of our time." Agca's own contradictory confessions have at times laid the blame on the Bulgarian government, acting at the behest of the KGB, and an Islamic conspiracy. CIA reports and various private investigators have alleged that Soviet authorities engineered the plot.

At this writing, nearly eighteen years since the assassination attempt, the case still evades conclusion for lack of evidence. "Surely the assassination was not an isolated attack," said Vatican State Secretary Cardinal Agostino Casaroli in 1995. Cardinal Achille Silvestrini, Casaroli's deputy at the time, said, "It was clear to us that it was . . . not simply the act of a madman. It was something aimed at a goal, there was something behind the killer. . . ."

Throughout the investigation, the pope has shown little interest in the findings. Agca, in interviews with journalists, has said, "The pope knows everything." At any rate, the Vatican has indicated that John Paul's interest lies not in who was behind the plot to end his life, but in who saved his life and why.

TOTUS TUUS, MARIA

"Totus Tuus [I am completely yours], Mary. This phrase is not only an expression of piety, or simply an expression of devotion. There is more," wrote John Paul II. Some Catholics find the pope's devotion to the Mother of God excessive, while some Protestants dismiss it as superstitious, unscriptural, and to some extent, blasphemous. Marian devotion, however, comes as naturally as daylight to John Paul II, something that springs, as he says, not only from a need of the human heart but from a lifelong reflection on the Divine Mother's role in the cosmic scheme of things. Then again, Karol Wojtyla owes much of it to the long history of Marian devotion in Poland.

The Divine Mother, for centuries, has been at the heart of Polish Catholicism and patriotism. The *Bogurodzica* (Mother of God), a hymn ascribed by tradition to St. Adalbert, first apostle of Poland, was sung on the eve of battles, and is still sung at the great shrines of Poland where millions flock every year.

When Warsaw was captured by the Swedes in 1655, Poles believed that it was the Virgin Mary who saved Poland at the Battle of Częstochowa. The Black Madonna of Częstochowa, a five-hundred-year-old icon housed in the Pauline Monastery on the hill of Jasna Góra, is the central symbol of Catholicism in Poland.

Many miracles have been attributed to the Black Madonna, notably the victory of a small band of monks and knights against the vastly superior Swedish army during the era of "The Deluge," when Poland was under attack from all directions. Legend has it that, at the moment the Swedish army was ready to fire its cannons at the monastery on Jasna Góra, the entire monastery rose from the ground and levitated above its attackers.

On April 1, 1656, King Jan Kazimierz dedicated Poland to Our Lady, Queen of Poland, an honor she retains to this day. (The consecration of Poland to Our Lady has been repeated at decisive moments of the nation's history, notably on August 26, 1956, the three hundredth anniversary of the Polish victory at Częstochowa. Over a million and a half Poles went to Jasna Góra, vowing to Our Lady to dedicate their individual lives, and that of Poland's, to divine will.)

To John Paul II, Marian devotion, as he wrote in *Crossing the Threshold of Hope*, "is not only a form of piety. . . it is also an attitude—an attitude toward woman as woman." In describing this attitude, the pope refers to the milieu in which he was brought up. "It was a time of great respect and consideration for women, especially for women who were mothers."

Mary, as the one who said yes to the divine plan, is recognized in the pope's writings as the one whose "union with God . . . exceeds all the expectations of the human spirit"—indeed, a capacity inherent in the nature of both women and men. In the pope's apostolic letter on women, titled *Mulieris Dignitatem*, he highlights the particular genius of women to birth a better world. Toward this end, "Mary herself and devotion to Mary, when lived out in all its fullness," he states, "becomes a powerful and creative inspiration."

In extolling the central role of women in bringing forth the union between God and humanity, John Paul II quotes from the closing message of the Second Vatican Council: "The hour is coming, in fact, has come, when the vocation of women is being acknowledged in its fullness, the hour in which women acquire in the world an influence, an effect, and a power never hitherto achieved."

OPPOSITE: *The Black Madonna, Our Lady of Częstochowa, is a Byzantine icon supposedly painted by St. Luke the Evangelist on a wooden plank that was the Holy Family's table at Nazareth. Legend has it that her face was slashed twice by the sword of a Hussite soldier during an invasion in 1430.*
ABOVE: *The Virgin Mary in a detail of Michelangelo's* Pietá.

That All May Be One

arriers between people of diverse faiths, as John Paul II's decades of ecumenical and interreligious efforts show, may be harder to tear down than the Berlin Wall. But this pope isn't one to lose hope.

He has crossed interfaith barriers in ways that no other pope has done. Above all, he has done it more in deed than in mere words. Centuries of painful conflicts with churches that broke away from the Roman Catholic faith have not daunted his efforts toward achieving unity—in spirit, if not in doctrine. The spirit of unity, in John Paul II and the Second Vatican Council's terms, is universal. It is fundamentally bound, not simply by a commonality of the world's religious beliefs but by humanity's "common roots" and "a common destiny."

John Paul II is the first pope to enter a synagogue, the first pope to enter the Canterbury Cathedral, and the first pope to preach in a Lutheran Church. He has been in continual dialogue with leaders of the world's religions in an effort to identify common grounds and ways to collaborate toward lasting peace. He speaks with a sense of urgency in calling people of all faiths to recognize the unity that is already present, and not to see differences as a cause for separation. He wrote in *Crossing the Threshold of Hope*, "This unity is enormously precious. In a certain sense, the future of the world is at stake."

In October 1986, John Paul II saw a perfect opportunity for collaboration among the world's religious leaders—to pray and fast for world peace. He called for a multifaith assembly in Assisi, home of St. Francis, one of Christianity's most beloved saints. At the time, disarmament negotiations between Ronald Reagan and Mikhail Gorbachev had just broken down, and the arms race resumed. Discouraged by this development, the pope looked to the power of prayer to influence world events. A few weeks before

the Assisi assembly, the pope called upon world leaders to observe a "universal truce." His appeal gathered widespread support, and fighting temporarily stopped in many of the world's current so-called hot spots. Countries not at war organized moments of prayer and meditation.

Meanwhile, in Assisi, the pope welcomed spiritual leaders, representing more than 450 million people and seventy-five religious denominations, including Buddhists, Hindus, Christians, Muslims, Sikhs, Zoroastrians, and members of traditional African and Native American religions. The assembly prayed and fasted for world peace, with each emissary praying in the language and manner of his or her own tradition.

OPPOSITE: *The pope speaks with Queen Elizabeth II during his visit to England in 1982. This visit also brought the pope together with the Anglican primate, Dr. Robert Runcie.*

ABOVE: *The pope receives the traditional nose kiss from a Maori elder during the Maori welcoming ceremonies in Auckland, New Zealand, on November 22, 1986.*

ABOVE: *The pope in Zaire, May 1980. He has often praised traditional African society for its "conception of a world in which the sacred occupies a central position." "Preserve your culture," he told Africans, "and offer it as your contribution to the world."*

OPPOSITE: *The fourteenth Dalai Lama and the pope have met several times over the years. Together with other leading world figures, they recently joined forces in the Jubilee 2000 Campaign for Western nations to write off Third World debts.*

"The challenge of peace," the pope said in Assisi, "transcends religious differences." As an act of penance, the pope, in his personal prayer, said, "I am ready to acknowledge that . . . [we Catholics] have not always been builders of peace." As the Cold War came to a surprisingly peaceful end a few years later, the pope came to believe that the multifaith prayer said in Assisi had, indeed, been answered.

While John Paul II has taken vigorous strides on the path of interfaith cooperation, his own Church has not kept up with its pontiff. In a 1994 editorial, the Jesuit periodical *America* commented that thirty years after the issue of the Second Vatican Council's Decree on Ecumenism, "it is not clear that the ecumenical promise of Vatican II has permeated the day-to-day workings of the Roman Catholic Church, nor that the optimism engendered by the council has been perpetuated even after many fruitful post-conciliar dialogues."

In citing the contributions of some of the world's great religions, Pope Paul VI, in *Nostra Aetate* (The Declaration on the Relation of the Church to Non-Christian Religions) proclaimed on October 28, 1965, "The Catholic Church rejects nothing that is true and holy in these religions. She regards with sincere reverence those ways of conduct and of life, those precepts and teachings which, though differing in many aspects from the ones she holds and sets forth, nonetheless often reflect a ray of Truth which enlightens all men." World religions, said John Paul II in the same spirit, possess "treasures of human spirituality" and implicitly enshrine those "seeds of the Gospel" of which the Fathers of the Church spoke.

The right-wing press has criticized the Church for having "sold out to ecumenism" and for bartering its soul for a mess "of ecumenical porridge." The fortress church, in the view of many

conservative Catholics, has become too much of a pilgrim church, and many more say they no longer know what the Church believes. John Paul II may disagree with such views, but he nonetheless encourages them to be aired in the open, lest they poison the inner life of the Church.

Since there can be no lasting world peace unless there is peace between religions, the pope urges people of all faiths to dialogue for dialogue's sake, with a constant view of the underlying unity shared by the world's religions. Without this view, he cautions, people fall into shortsightedness, a key ingredient of insular, fundamentalist belief. Whatever its stripe, fundamentalism—in its myriad expressions of intolerance—has been a major roadblock to interfaith harmony.

"As old barriers fall, new ones arise whenever fundamental truths and values are forgotten or obscured, even among people who profess themselves to be religious," John Paul II said at the World Conference on Religion and Peace held at the Vatican early in November 1994.

In one of his most important pronouncements, the pope said at the conference, "Today, religious leaders must clearly show that they are pledged to the promotion of peace precisely because of their religious belief. Religion is not, and must not become, a pretext for conflict, particularly when religious, cultural, and ethnic identity collide . . . . Religion and peace go together: to wage war in the name of religion is a blatant contradiction."

Interfaith collaboration, the pope said, "must never mean a reduction to a common minimum," and must be a challenge for each religion to keep clear its unique place and purpose in the universal scheme of things. A reverence for diversity, in his view, is inherent in universal communion.

In the encyclical *Dominum et Vivificantem*, John Paul II looked to ecumenical unity to help restore the force of religion in an increasingly materialistic world. "We must convince ourselves of the ethical over the technical," the pope said in a speech at UNESCO, "of the person over things, of the . . . spiritual over the material."

John Paul II the philosopher refers to the work of the philosophers of dialogue, Martin Buber and Emmanuel Lévinas, in navigating the complex landscape of interfaith encounters. The path of dialogue, the pope wrote, "is not so much through being and existence as through people and their meeting each other," through the human and the sovereign *Thou*—which is a *"fundamental dimension of man's existence, which is always a coexistence."*

Personal contact, stresses the pope, is ever so important in bridging religious division: "I grow more convinced of this every time I meet leaders of various religions, whether in Rome or in visits to various parts of the world."

John Paul II's journey on the road of interfaith dialogue has been frequently strewn with obstacles, as age-old schisms persist and doctrinal differences overshadow the promise of cooperation. He is, however, no respecter of obstacles, and enjoins everyone *". . . to rid ourselves of stereotypes, of old habits*. And above all, it is necessary to *recognize the unity that already exists."*

OPPOSITE: *John Paul II was the first pope to praise Martin Luther (pictured) as
a visionary and to preach in a Lutheran church.*

ABOVE AND RIGHT: *The pope's travels have made his face one of the most
recognizeable of the twentieth century. His warmth and charisma have touched
and inspired Catholics and non-Catholics alike all over the world.*

ABOVE: *The pope in Britain in 1982. Willing to travel far and wide, able to speak eleven languages, and possessing a casual, down-to-earth style, John Paul II quickly established himself as the people's pope.*
OPPOSITE: *The formality of the papacy had made previous popes seem completely inaccessible; yet even amid the pomp of a High Mass, John Paul II exudes a sense of warmth and humanity.*

The Pilgrim Pope

Cold War's End

The Pope? And how many divisions does the Pope have?" Joseph Stalin once mockingly asked. Decades later, the reply to Stalin's question would haunt his successors. The pope, indeed, had divisions— not the battalions that Stalin meant, of course, but the ordinary citizens who forged the nonviolent mass movement against communism.

When General Wojciech Jaruzelski, the last communist to rule Poland, was asked when the Polish revolution began, he replied, "In 1979, when John Paul II visited Poland for the first time." Under the watchful eyes of communist authorities, the visit drew millions, consolidating an unprecedented measure of hope and strength among the faithful.

An editorial in the London Catholic newspaper *The Tablet* had this to say on the pope's 1979 visit to Poland: "Never before in Christian history has the world seen such a confrontation of spiritual force and material power as in the pope's first visit to Poland. One man came to a state surrounded and dominated by the most formidable militant atheistic regime that has ever existed, armed with every weapon. . . . Had he been a local prophet with the same vision and message, he might have been bundled away into a forced labor camp. . . . But the pope walked into a tyranny which could not touch him. . . . One man seems to have demonstrated what manhood means."

In 1980, shortly after the visit, the Solidarity Movement was born, as a local shipyard strike in Gdansk. As Solidarity grew, it began to inspire anticommunist movements across eastern and central Europe. The pope's "divisions"—some fifty million Roman Catholics in eastern Europe, including thirty-five million in Poland, and more than four million in the Soviet Union itself—began to organize in peaceful protest. Solidarity leader Lech Walesa stated, "Without the pope's work and prayer . . . there would be no Solidarity."

The Solidarity model of nonviolent resistance—the building of an extensive network of workers and intellectuals, combined with the weight of moral authority—took the world by surprise when it overcame Soviet forces without the use of arms. Communist regimes in eastern and central Europe collapsed without bloodshed like a row of dominoes.

BELOW: *Pope John Paul II with Solidarity leader Lech Walesa (left). Even as the pope gave his support to Solidarity, Walesa stated that "Solidarity is not the Church, and the Church is not Solidarity."*

ABOVE: *The pope with U.S. Secretary of State Henry Kissinger, one of those who believed that the Soviets were probably behind the assassination attempt on the pope. Kissinger also asserted that the U.S.S.R. "will be a totalitarian state" even after the completion of Mikhail Gorbachev's reforms.*

On December 1, 1989, Soviet president Mikhail Gorbachev met with John Paul II in the Vatican. "As I watched their ceremonial encounter," recounts author Fred Coleman in *The Decline and Fall of the Soviet Empire*, "I could hardly believe my eyes. It was logical to expect one day that a Soviet leader might improve relations with the United States, with China, even Germany. But communism was a secular religion, with its own self-proclaimed monopoly on truth, an implacable foe of everything the Roman Catholic Church stood for. . . . And yet, there it was. The words of reconciliation they exchanged struck me as particularly significant."

"The Holy See follows with great interest the process of renewal which you set in motion in the Soviet Union," the pope told President Gorbachev during the historic meeting of these two powerful leaders. "It wishes you success and declares itself ready to support every initiative that will better protect and integrate the rights and duties of individuals and people, so that peace may be ensured in Europe and the world."

"We have changed our attitude on some matters, such as religion," Gorbachev replied, "which admittedly we used to treat in a simplistic manner. Now we not only proceed from the assumption that no one should interfere in matters of the individual's conscience, we also say that the moral values that religion embodied for centuries, such as goodness, mercy, and mutual aid, can help in the work of renewal of our country, too. In fact, this is already happening."

On December 8, 1991, the presidents and prime ministers of Russia, Ukraine, and Belarus declared the U.S.S.R. dissolved and founded a Commonwealth of Independent States. On December 25, Gorbachev resigned. On December 31, the Soviet Union ceased to exist. The Cold War had ended.

After the demise of the U.S.S.R., Gorbachev wrote in 1992, "Everything that happened in Eastern Europe during these past few years would have been impossible without the pope, without the political role he was able to play. . . . His philosophy and patient actions made a new kind of thinking possible for us all."

When the world came to hail John Paul II for being the single most important figure in the demise of the Cold War, he responded by discouraging his audiences from oversimplifying the matter or even attributing the collapse of the Soviet empire to the hand of God. "I didn't cause it to happen," he stated. "The tree was already rotten. I just gave it a good shake and the rotten apples fell." He further stated that the fall of communism was not about the victory of one ideology over another, but about inherent weaknesses in a system that bode inevitable change.

"The pope gave form to the revolt that was coming," Adam Krzemiński, a Polish intellectual, wrote in the newspaper *Politika*. "He civilized and tamed it from the inside."

While most Western observers saw John Paul II as playing an intensely political role in the dismantling of communist rule in Europe, journalist Lawrence Weschler noted in *The Passion of Poland* that a close reading of his eastern European addresses shows that he called not for revolt but for "truth, freedom, and justice," and always, at the same time, "for love, reconciliation, and peace."

ABOVE: *The pope with Wojciech Jaruzelski, the last communist to rule Poland before the end of the Cold War. Jaruzelski's regime gave way to Solidarity without violence.*
BELOW: *Fidel Castro greets John Paul II after the pope's historic visit to Havana's Plaza of the Revolution Square on January 25, 1998. At the climactic papal Mass in the square, chants of "Freedom, Freedom" from the three hundred thousand people in attendance rang out as Castro looked on.*

The Pilgrim Pope   83

ABOVE: *The Berlin Wall comes down. The painful scar on the face of Europe gives way to unity.*

ABOVE: *On September 17, 1993, during his first trip to the countries of the former U.S.S.R., the pope walks by the "Hill of Crosses" on his way to celebrate an outdoor Mass in Siauliai, Lithuania. Thousands of crosses were erected by Lithuanians in defiance of the communist Soviet regime.*

Chapter Five
The Watershed Pope

Splendor of Truth

erhaps the greatest challenge of John Paul II's papacy, after the dismantling of communist rule in Europe, has been the moral crisis in Western society. Like many people, the pope believes that a profound moral shift has taken place in the twentieth century, not only in the West but in many parts of the world—a change that has devalued the institution that John Paul II has proclaimed to be the heart of human civilization—the family.

The family, John Paul wrote in his *Letter to Families*, ". . . is placed at the center of the great struggle between good and evil, between life and death, between love and all that is opposed to love."

The latest statistics are a telling blow to John Paul II's pontificate on the sanctity of the family. In the United States alone, half of all marriages ended in divorce, up from 21 percent in the first half of the century. In many cities, the number of unwanted pregnancies continues to rise; these often end in abortion, or in the birth of a child whose mother or father is unprepared for the responsibilities of parenthood.

In his economics encyclical, *Centesimus Annus* (The Hundredth

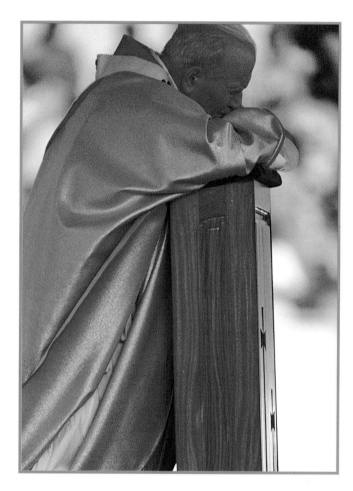

PAGE 86: *Pope John Paul II's warm smile and charasmatic manner made him instantly popular.*
PAGE 87: Crucifixion with the Virgin, and Saints John the Evangelist and Peter and Paul. *Juan de Borgona, c. 1510. North Carolina Museum of Art.*
ABOVE: *The pope kneels on a* prie dieu, *absorbed in prayer. Aides have often found the pope lost in prayer for more than an hour, sometimes lying prostrate on a cold marble floor.*
OPPOSITE: *Troubled by the high rates of divorce, abortion, and unwanted pregnancies in Western society, the pope has urged a recognition of what he calls the sanctity of the family.*

Anniversary, alluding to Pope Leo XIII's *Rerum Novarum* in 1891), the pope wrote, "It is necessary to go back to seeing the family as the sanctuary of life. The family is indeed sacred: it is the place in which life—the gift of God—can be properly welcomed and protected against the many attacks to which it is exposed."

John Paul II has taken to task both the economic and political forces that he believes undermine the "rights of the family." Speaking at a youth rally in Paris, the pope cited the misgivings of communist and capitalist societies alike in putting undue pressure on parents to bring in more and more money, often at the expense of their families. He called for "the rights of the family" to be deeply inscribed "in every code of work."

Every effort should be made, declared the pope, to uphold and preserve the integrity of the family, "for a truly sovereign and spiritually vigorous nation is always made up of strong families who are aware of their vocation and mission in history." It is not an exaggeration to reaffirm, the pope declared, that the life of states, of nations, and indeed of the world at large is dependent on upholding the family.

With the breakdown of families, the postmodern age has seen the rise of moral relativism, a developement that John Paul II has dealt with in no uncertain terms. In the pope's encyclical on fundamental moral values, *Veritatis Splendor* (The Splendor of Truth), a point is made that moral values have, as their basis, natural law, as well as divine revelation, which is enshrined in the human heart.

In *Veritatis*, the pope pointed out "the risk of an alliance between democracy and ethical relativism." Such alliance, he explained, "would remove any sure moral reference point from political and social life and, on a deeper level, make the acknowledgment of truth impossible. Indeed, if there is no ultimate truth to guide and direct political activity, then ideas and convictions can be easily manipulated for reasons of power. As history demonstrates, a democracy without values easily turns into open or thinly disguised totalitarianism."

Commenting on *Veritatis Splendor*, Arthur John Anderson, Jr., former director of the Criminal Justice Division in Little Rock, Arkansas, and former teaching fellow at Harvard Law School, said, "Where there is much moral deterioration, John Paul II is a voice in the wilderness. What has happened is . . . instead of living our lives around truth, we create our own truths to accommodate our lives. The pope is saying that there is truth, and that truth is the reference point." Rev. Mr. Anderson, who's now a Roman Catholic deacon based in Ottumwa, Iowa, adds, "John Paul II is a guidepost. He is an anchor."

When the capacity to know the truth is darkened, John Paul II has stated, the will to submit to truth is also weakened, "but no darkness of error or of sin can totally take away from man the light of God the Creator. In the depths of his heart there always remains a yearning for absolute truth and a thirst to attain full knowledge of it."

ABOVE: *The pope signs his latest encyclical,* **Fides et Ratio** *(Faith and Reason), on October 15, 1998. The encyclical notes that the world is moving so fast that many people no longer stop to ask the meaning of life and risk losing their souls to the very technology they have come to worship.*

OPPOSITE: *The pope embraces two children who came to greet him upon his arrival in Baltimore, Maryland, on October 8, 1995. Through the years, John Paul II has never missed an appointment with youth on World Youth Day, his pet project. Children are a great source of hope to him.*

ABOVE: *The pope greets children as he walks about town in Denmark. The "people's pope" has transformed the image of the papacy from an ivory-tower figure to a globe-trotting pilgrim.*

OPPOSITE: *The pope and U.S. President William Clinton are on their way to make joint statements after their private one-hour meeting at Regis University in Denver, Colorado, on August 12, 1993. Over the years, the two leaders have wrestled with the abortion question.*

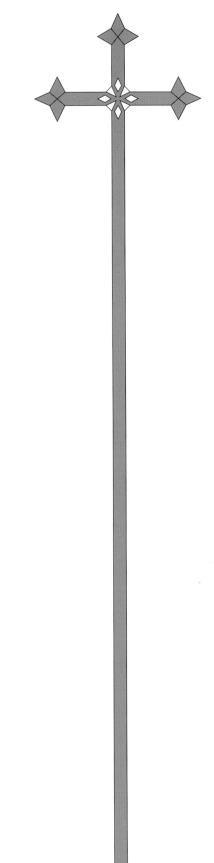

ABOVE: *The papal limousine sweeps through Warsaw. The city, which saw 200,000 of its citizens butchered by Nazis during the Warsaw Uprising, is jubilant at the return of Poland's pilgrim of peace.*

ABOVE: *The pope waves to a crowd gathered at Nairobi, Kenya. John Paul II has had to face the challenge of reconciling Kenya's population problem with the Church's ban on artificial birth control.*

"How many Popes, Holy Father, who possessed the same Office as Your Holiness, but not the same intelligence or greatness of mind and spirit . . . have permitted the ruin and destruction of antique temples, statues, arches, and other buildings resounding to the glory of their founders?" wrote Raphael and Baldassare Castiglione to Pope Leo X.

John Paul II would not be one to permit the ruin of Michelangelo's masterpiece—the frescoes of the Sistine Chapel—which had deteriorated under nearly five hundred years of soot and grime.

The pope commissioned the restoration of the Sistine Chapel in 1981, a painstaking task that took fourteen years to complete. The restoration of the ceiling frescoes was completed in 1989; the *Last Judgment* in 1995. Amid much controversy, many experts agree that Michelangelo could not complain about the restoration. It has, in their opinion, revealed the work in its true glory, and it has shed new light on its creator.

Between 1508 and 1512, Michelangelo labored on the ceiling of the Sistine Chapel at the behest of Pope Julius II. He accepted the task with great reluctance, reasoning that he was a sculptor, not a painter. Michelangelo, nonetheless, undertook the work with great passion and purpose, creating one of the greatest works of art of all time.

Twenty-two years after the completion of the ceiling frescoes, Pope Paul III commanded Michelangelo to paint the *Last Judgment* on the altar wall of the Sistine. When the work was unveiled in 1541, the awed pope sank to his knees in prayer. Many people, however, were disturbed by the naked figures on the fresco. One critic remarked that the *Last Judgment* "did not belong in a papal chapel, but in public baths or brothels."

When pressure to alter the fresco grew intolerable, the succeeding pope, Paul IV, sent word to Michelangelo "to tidy up" the fresco. The defiant artist replied, "Tell the Pope that this is a small matter and it can very easily be tidied up. In the meantime, let him tidy up the world, for pictures are readily tidied up."

The Council of Trent (1545) settled the dispute by ordering that the naked figures be clothed. Between 1565, a year after Michelangelo's death, and the late eighteenth century, forty-one figures were covered. Before the *Last Judgment*'s restoration began, a decision was made, after much debate, that the modern-day restorers would remove most of the coverings. As an historical note, the coverings that were done as a direct result of the Council of Trent were retained.

The restoration, through computer analysis, revealed that painter Daniele da Volterra, who did some of the coverings, had trouble matching the green of St. Catherine's dress in the *Last Judgment*. Restorer Bruno Baratti remarked, "The spirit of Michelangelo came back and switched paint pots with him."

RIGHT: *Michelangelo Buonarotti's (1475–1564)* The Last Judgement *as it appeared before the restoration of the Sistine Chapel.*

On Science and Religion

For centuries, science and religion, in some minds, have been at odds with each other—a situation that John Paul II sees as a "needless conflict." Given the Church's history of putting to trial some of her scientific sons and daughters, the pope, himself a patron of the sciences, sees it as one of his great duties to help clear the confusion that has marred the relationship between the two monumental human disciplines.

Within a month of his election, John Paul II lost no time in proposing that the Church make amends for forcing the Italian astronomer Galileo Galilei to recant his claim that the sun, not the earth, as opposed to scriptural claim, was the center of the solar system. (This was one step in a much broader effort to explore the relationship between science and religion, and to put a close to Old Testament fundamentalist views of science.)

Although the Church admitted, as far back as 1741, that Galileo was right by granting an imprimatur for the publication of his writings, it never publicly acknowledged that it had erred in trying him in court in 1633. Three and a half centuries later, in 1992, the Vatican formally pronounced Galileo innocent of charges brought against him by the Inquisition. "The greatness of Galileo is recognized by all," John Paul II said, "but we cannot deny that he suffered greatly at the hands of churchmen and church bodies."

In Galileo's time, the conflict, John Paul II pointed out, had to do with theologians' insistence on literal interpretations of Scripture. He quoted a letter Galileo wrote to Christine of Lauren: "Scripture can never lie, provided one understands its meaning, which is often hidden and very different from what the plain meaning of the words might suggest." On this, the pope gave credit to Galileo's good sense to interpret Scripture in a manner "which goes beyond the literal sense, but which attends to the

intentions of the author and the literary form in which they are couched."

Advancing the cause of science is, to John Paul II, an important function of the Church. Every year, he plays host to leading scientists who come to Castel Gandolfo for a three-day science seminar whose sessions he attends in earnest. Through his encouragement, the Vatican observatory published in 1993 a 450-page book, *Quantum Creation of the Universe and the Origin of the Laws of Nature*. When the lights of Rome began to interfere with sky watching from the Vatican Observatory, the pope commissioned a new observatory in Arizona.

In 1988, after the pope-sponsored "Study Week" at the Vatican observing the three hundredth anniversary of Sir Isaac Newton's

Principia Mathematica, John Paul II wrote a lengthy letter to Vatican Observatory director, Father George Coyne. The letter articulates the pope's insights on the complementary roles that science and religion can play in the search for truth. He wrote, "Religion is not founded on science, nor is science an extension of religion. . . . While each can and should support the other as distinct dimensions of a common human culture, neither ought to assume that it forms a necessary premise for the other. . . . Science can purify religion from idolatry and false absolutes. Each can draw the other into the wider world . . . in which both can flourish."

OPPOSITE: *The pope appointed a commission to reinvestigate the 350-year-old case of Galileo Galilei (1564–1642), the Italian physicist and astronomer who was threatened with burning unless he renounced his theory that the earth revolved around the sun.*

RIGHT: *Pope John Paul II takes a break during a skiing trip to do a little reading. His reflections on the natural world have inspired a renaissance of scientific inquiry at the Vatican.*

At a youth rally in Paris, John Paul II was asked to identify the most crucial issue regarding peace and justice in the world. He declared that the paramount issue was the moral obligation of rich countries toward poor countries. The gap between rich and poor people—and countries—he said, could not be permitted to stand or widen. In his encyclical *Sollicitudo Rei Socialis* (On Social Concerns), the pope wrote that development either becomes shared by every part of the world or undergoes regression in zones marked by constant progress: "Either all the nations of the world [must] participate or it will not be true development."

True development, John Paul II said, "cannot consist in the simple accumulation of wealth and the greater availability of goods and services, if this is gained at the expense of the development of the masses, and without due consideration for the social, cultural, and spiritual dimensions of the human being."

Materialistic Western society, the pope explained to journalist André Frossard, "aims to convince man that he is . . . adapted to the structure of the visible world." The great danger, he added, is "cutting man off from his own depths."

The culture of competition and consumption promoted by the West, he wrote in *Sollicitudo*, has been promoting ideals that fall far short of genuine human development. "Side by side with the miseries of underdevelopment, themselves unacceptable, we find ourselves up against a form of super-development, equally inadmissible, [which] easily makes people slaves of possession and immediate gratification, with no other horizon than the continual replacement of the things already owned with others still better." An object is discarded, wrote the pope, with little or no thought of its possible lasting value, nor of another human being who is poorer and might claim its value is still apparent.

"This then is the picture," wrote John Paul II. "There are some people—the few who possess much—who do not really succeed in 'being' because, through a reversal of the hierarchy of values, they are hindered by the cult of 'having,' and there are others—the many who have little or nothing—who do not succeed in realizing their basic human vocation because they are deprived of essential goods."

When individuals and communities do not observe a rigorous respect for moral, cultural, and spiritual requirements based on the dignity of the person, wrote the pope, then all material progress will prove unsatisfying and, in the end, contemptible.

Further, John Paul II stated that development must never exclude respect for the natural world, as one must take into account the nature of each living being and its mutual connection in an ordered system.

OPPOSITE, LEFT: *The Holy Father with Mother Teresa. When the pope visited Mother Teresa's hospice in Calcutta, he personally comforted the sick and the dying, some of whom grabbed his hand and held it to their faces.*
OPPOSITE, RIGHT: *The pope offers communion to a man on crutches during a trip to France. He champions the spiritual over the material, as he fights for economic justice.*
RIGHT: *The pope deep in prayer on a visit to Lombardy, France, in 1992. John Paul II has addressed economic injustice in prayer and action.*

Mea Culpa, Mea Culpa

ea culpa, mea culpa for the Church's past sins, of both commission and omission. The Inquisition. The Repression of Protestantism. The overzealousness of the Crusades. Christian war crimes. The history of the Church includes terrible deeds, and though it may be painful, Pope John Paul II wants it all unburied, to be reflected upon and never to be repeated.

"The sins of the past still burden us," the pope said in 1994, as he outlined plans for the Church's Jubilee 2000 celebration. He issued letters urging all members of the Church to reexamine and repent for sins and crimes committed by Catholics in past centuries.

Against the advice of cardinals opposed to the enormous complexity of digging through two thousand years of history and performing a public act of penance, John Paul II appointed a team of scholars to catalog the Church's misdeeds and help lay a factual foundation for genuine self-examination.

In a memorandum sent to cardinals all over the world, the pope wrote: "How can we keep silent about all the forms of violence that have been perpetrated in the name of faith? About the wars of religion, the inquisitorial tribunals, and other ways of violating the rights of the individual? It is significant that these coercive methods, which violate human rights, have subse-

quently been applied by the totalitarian ideologies of the twentieth century. . . . The Church, too, must make an independent review of the darker sides of its history."

During the unprecedented Vatican symposium in November 1998, the pope called on the Church to ponder how the Inquisition's

"methods of intolerance and even violence in the service of truth" fell short of the Gospel. The symposium is part of a concerted effort that the pope has called a "purification of memory."

In a sixteen thousand–word apostolic letter issued in November of 1994, the pope told Catholics that the Church "cannot cross the threshold of the new millennium without encouraging her children to purify themselves, through repentance of past errors. . . ." Through such purification, the pope anticipates that old wounds may heal at last.

OPPOSITE: *Bearing the burden of his Church's past sins, John Paul II prays for purification and forgiveness.*
BELOW: *The pope lights a candle in prayer. After the demise of the Soviet Union, the pope grappled with Eastern Europe's wrenching transition into a free market and the rising materialism in the newly liberated republics.*

CONCLUSION

The Easter Pope

The life of Karol Josef Wojtyla, as many of his biographers have concluded, has defined our age in a way that perhaps no other man's has. He is paid a common tribute, one that Bernstein and Politi, in *His Holiness*, have stated well: "The world has become aware that he is the last of the giants on the global stage—that there are no other great heralds of broad vision or principle, whatever their cause or ideology. He has defined his time as perhaps no other leader has, even while railing against the age itself."

John Paul II has reigned longer than all but 18 of the 262 previous popes. And as the Church celebrates its two-thousandth birthday at the turn of the millennium, he looks forward with great hope and anticipation. "Be not afraid!" he has been telling his flock from the onset of his papacy, well aware of the enormous challenges that not only he and his Church face but the world at large as well.

It is the same message given by the Angel Gabriel to Mary, by Christ to the apostles, by St. Augustine to the people of Hippo. Just as St. Augustine kept reassuring his people, "This is not an old world dying. But a new world being born," so John Paul II, through his life and work, has offered a vision of faith in the capacity of the human spirit to conquer fear, love's greatest foe.

PAGE 104: *The pope looks out into the crowd during "The Light of the World" youth rally in St. Louis, Missouri, January 26, 1999.*
PAGE 105: *The stunning interior of the dome of St. Peter's Basilica.*
ABOVE: *John Paul II greets crowds in St. Louis. The pope's first speech in St. Louis expresses his friendship and esteem for his fellow Christians, the Jewish community, the Muslim community, and for all people of all religions and for every person of goodwill.*
OPPOSITE: *The pope holds his staff during a prayer inside the Trans World Dome in St. Louis, Missouri, on January 27, 1999, where he celebrated Mass before a congregation of 80,000.*

"Does man reveal himself in thinking, or, rather, in the actual enacting of his existence?" Karol Josef wrote in *The Acting Person*, his anthropological work that underlines the importance of the actions of each individual in the universal scheme of things. "Reality," he said, is "in the confrontation itself, when [man] has to take an active stand . . . having vital consequences and repercussions."

The pope of action has demonstrated, in no small way, the power of the transcendent approach in shaping history. When the world could not see a peaceful end to the Cold War, John Paul II sparked a revolution, not by inciting his people to arms but by letting them recognize their own dignity and the need to uphold it by all means, except, of course, the violent.

"He told us to first deal with ourselves, and to see ourselves as one, regardless of our ideologies," recalls Father Adam Barcz who, in his youth, was present at all of John Paul II's pilgrimages to Poland before the end of the Cold War. "The 1970s were a very dark time for the Polish people," reflects Barcz, now a pastor in Oregon. "It was difficult to see through the darkness. Then came John Paul II. After his first visit in Poland, Solidarity was formed. It inspired others throughout Eastern

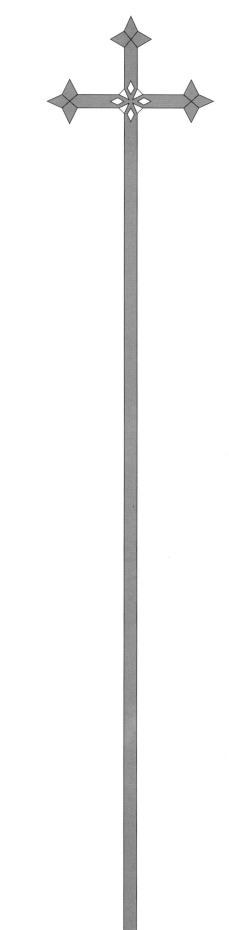

added, "Your Holiness, I do not know what a miracle is. Nevertheless, I dare say at this moment that I am party to a miracle. A man who only six months ago was taken prisoner as an enemy of his own state is welcoming today, as president, the first pope to set foot in Czechoslovakia. For long decades, the spirit has been chased out of our homeland. I have the honor to be a witness when its soil is kissed by the Apostle of Spirituality."

Although John Paul II's papacy had been largely defined in the context of the Cold War, his post–Cold War pontificate has been marked with greater challenges. Whatever the challenge, John Paul II's response has been in step with the goal of creating a civilization of love. To some, this goal—a world in which war will have given way to peace, greed to charity, separation to unity—is an unattainable utopia. But love, he states clearly, "is not a utopia." The pope wrote in his *Letter to Families*, "Love . . . is given to mankind as a task to be carried out with the help of divine grace."

This task has consumed Karol Wojtyla to the far limits of his mortality. The robustness has, in recent years, given way to increasing frailty. Certainly health setbacks—the bullet from the 1981 assassination attempt, colon surgery in 1992 to remove a precancerous tumor, a broken arm and a dislocated shoulder from a fall in 1993, and a broken leg and hip surgery from slipping in the bathtub in 1994—have not helped.

These physical challenges have not dampened the pope's willpower and prodigious creative output. In fact, a burst of activity characterizes the later years of his papacy, during which he has produced some of his most profound writings and most ambitious projects, including the Jubilee marking the turn of the millennium, the two thousandth birthday of Christ.

To many, the significance of the Jubilee is unclear. To John Paul II, however, it is—it must be—a clarion call for a turning

and Central Europe. Then what had seemed an impossibility became a reality. . . . The Cold War came to an end without bloodshed."

When John Paul II visited newly independent Czechoslovakia in 1990, Vaclav Havel, its new president, declared as soon as the pope had kissed the ground, "The Messenger of Love comes today into a country devastated by the ideology of hatred." Havel, who had served five years in prison under the communist regime, point for humanity. John Paul II's poetry, more so than his other writings, gives a glimpse of a prophetic vein at work, in various instances pointing to a time when the veil of ignorance and strife will, at last, be lifted.

Karol Josef Wojtyla's poetic pen has, since his election to the papacy, given way to addressing a host of contemporary issues. By 1998, John Paul II had written thirteen encyclicals and volumes of major documents in the form of letters and exhortations, with subjects ranging from labor and economics to the metaphysics of morality. He also wrote a best-seller, *Crossing the Threshold of Hope*, guided the creation of the best-selling *Catechism of the Catholic Church*, and recorded a recital of prayers, which ascended the charts in Europe.

John Paul II has reigned not as an administrator but as a globe-trotting pilgrim, eager to make personal contact with people around the world, whether they're in accord with him or not. By early 1999, John Paul II—who by then spoke 14 languages—had made more than 70 foreign trips, visiting over 110 countries. He had met with more than 510 heads of state and 150 prime ministers. Before embarking on one of his trips, John Paul II was asked by a journalist about the growing concern that he was traveling too much. The pope smiled, responding, "Yes, I am convinced that I am traveling too much. But, sometimes, it is necessary to do some things too much."

At last count, the pope had canonized 280 new saints, four times as many saints as all previous twentieth-century popes have canonized. "Man is called to victory over himself," he declared. "It is the saints and the beatified who show us the path of victory that God achieves in human history."

OPPOSITE: *Pink sunset during the papal coronation at St. Peter's Basilica. Despite health trials, John Paul II vigorously leads his Church to the next millennium.*
RIGHT: *The pope during St. Louis trip. During this trip, John Paul II reiterates the need for a higher moral vision in this time of great trials.*

The pope of reforms, to the frustration of many Catholics and non-Catholics alike, is also a pope of unbending regard for some of the Church's time-honored traditions. He has stood firm over such issues as priesthood celibacy, the ordination of women, artificial birth control, and abortion. He has explained, in a slew of encyclicals and apostolic letters, the basis for the Church's stand on these issues—and, as the pilgrim church would have it, the debate rages on. As John Paul II is wont to say, "Fear not"—even with regard to the pains of discourse.

Whether it's artificial birth control, nuclear arms, or racism that John Paul II speaks about, his rule of thumb in assessing issues—the supreme sanctity of human life—applies. When journalist Wilton Wynn asked the pope how he could categorically apply Christian doctrine to matters seemingly far removed from the domain of religion and morality, John Paul II replied, "We emphasize the transcendental worth of the human person. Some modern scientific and medical developments are apt to make the human person a product, an object. We insist that the human person must never be treated as an object; he must always be considered the subject. That is the basis of our teaching, the absolute standard."

In reflecting upon the impact of John Paul II on global affairs, Vytautas Landsbergis, a non-Catholic who became independent Lithuania's first president in 1990, told journalist Robin Wright, "What would the world be like without the pope? . . . I have said sometimes that it

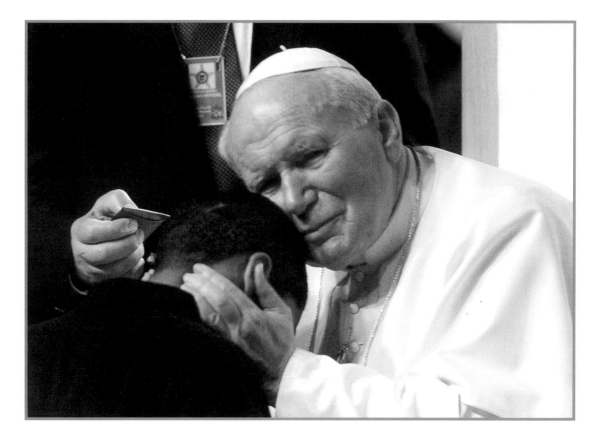

seems all Western leaders are Marxists. No one, with a very small exception, is speaking about spiritual problems. The only sphere of problems is economic effectiveness, zones of influence, and control in a rather materialistic way of being."

On a world stage dominated by profound economic, national, and religious divisions, John Paul II, as quoted by Bernstein and Politi, "stands out as the only international spokesperson for universal values." He offers a vision of hope and salvation in the face of the new idols—tribal egoism, exacerbated nationalism, fiercely sectarian and violent fundamentalism, and profit with no concern for its consequences.

To comprehend the journey of John Paul II is to know that he has walked into the eye of the storm of our age—a storm characterized by the fact that, in the postmodern world, as Havel put it, everything is possible, and almost nothing is certain. "Experts can explain anything in the objective world, yet we understand our own lives less and less."

In a very human, albeit magnified way, John Paul II has grappled with the essential challenges confronting humanity in a time of great change—to be at home away from home, to be still in action as in prayer and meditation, to uphold the Absolute in the relative world, to have certitude in a time of uncertainty, to lead and to be led, to be in the world but not of the world. John Paul II has confronted these challenges, not without difficulty, but always with grace and courage. In so doing, he has inspired a vision of unity and reconciliation in the world. Indeed, as papal biographer Tad Szulc has written, to know John Paul II, even slightly, is sufficient to sense that "he is at peace with himself, his God, and his world. . . ."

OPPOSITE, TOP: *Baseball hero Mark McGwire kisses the pope's ring before a youth rally at the Kiel Center in St. Louis, Missouri. McGwire, who was raised Catholic, set a major league record with seventy home runs in the 1998 season, and has been an inspiration for American youth.*

OPPOSITE, BOTTOM: *John Paul II embraces a child during a youth rally at the Kiel Center. "Train yourself in devotion," the pope told the crowd. "Use well the gifts the Lord has given you. You are the light of the world . . . Your light must shine before all (Mt 5:14–16)."*

ABOVE: *Pope John Paul II in prayer during a service in which France's Claudine Therent and Chilian Teresa de Jesus were canonized on March 21, 1993. The pope has been unfazed by criticism of his saint-making process, which has crowded the Catholic calendar. There are now more saints than days in a year.*

RIGHT: *The pope bestows a blessing as twenty-seven archbishops attend a ceremony to mark the feast of saints Peter and Paul at St. Peter's Basilica on June 29, 1993. Today's Vatican was built on the spot where early Christians said they buried Peter, the first pope, in about 64 A.D.*

LEFT: The pope celebrates the ordination of new bishops during the Mass on the Feast of Epiphany in St. Peter's Basilica at the Vatican on January 6, 1998. The new bishops brought the total around the world to 4,375.

Timeline: Events in the Life of His Holiness Pope John Paul II

1920
- May 18. Born Karol Josef Wojtyla in Wadowice, Poland, to Karol Wojtyla and Emilia Kaczorowska. Lived with his parents at Rynek 2 (now Via Koscielna 7, Apt. no. 4).

1926
- September 15. Entered elementary school for boys, and then prep years of secondary school at Marcin Wadowita. Achieved top grades in all classes.

1929
- April 13. Mother dies.

1930
- June. Admitted to the State Secondary School for boys.

1932
- December 5. Brother, Edmund, dies.

1935
- September. Participates in military training exercises at Hermanice.
- December 14. Admitted into the Society of Mary.

1938
- From 1934–1938. First student theatrical performances in Wadowice. During secondary school, he is president of the Society of Mary. First pilgrimage to Częstochowa.
- Summer. He and his father move to Kraków (Via Tyniecka 10).
- June 22. Enrolls at the Jagiellonian University, Kraków, to study Polish philology and literature.
- Beginning of Academic Year. Joins the "Studio 39" experimental theater group founded by Tadeusz Kudlinski.

1939
- September. Second World War begins.

1940
- February. Meets spiritual mentor Jan Tryanowski.
- October. Earns living as a stone cutter at a Solvay Plant quarry in Zakrzówek, Kraków.

1941
- February 18. Father dies.

1941–1944
- Took part in all of seven wartime productions of the Rhapsodic Theater Company.

1942
- Spring. Transferred to the Solvay chemical plant.
- October. Begins clandestine studies for the priesthood in Kraków's underground seminary.

1944
- February 29–March 12. Hit by a truck, recovery in hospital.

- August. Transferred, together with other clandestine seminarians, to Archbishop Adam Stefan Sapieha's Residence. Continues studies but not work at Solvay.
- January 18. Russian Armed Forces free Kraków from Nazi occupation.

1945
- April 9. Elected vice-president of the student organization *Bratnia Pomoc* (Fraternal Help) at Jagiellonian University.

1946
- November 1. Ordained a priest.
- November 2. Celebrates first Mass.
- November 15. Leaves Poland to begin studies in Rome.
- November 26. Registers at the Angelicum University.

1947
- July 3. Earns a licentiate in theology.

1948
- June 14–19. Defends thesis, "The Questions of Faith in the Works of St. John of the Cross" and earns a doctorate in philosophy.
- Sent as assistant pastor to Niegowic near Gdów.
- December 16. Earns master's degree in theology at the Theological Faculty of Jagiellonian University.

1949
- February. Earns doctorate in Sacred Theology at the Jagiellonian University on the basis of an expanded text of his Angelicum dissertation on St. John of the Cross.
- Recalled to Kraków to be assistant pastor at St. Florian's Parish.

1951
- September 1. Archbishop Eugeniusz Baziak puts him on leave until 1953 to complete his qualifying exams for a university position.

1953
- From October. Gives a course in Catholic social ethics at Jagiellonian University.
- December 1–3. Presents doctoral dissertation, "Building a System of Christian Ethics Based on Max Scheler's Philosophy," to the Theological Faculty of Jagiellonian University. Could not be awarded his second doctorate degree as the communist regime refused to grant academic degrees to priests.

1954
- Faculty of Theology at Jagiellonian University abolished. Accepts professorship at the Catholic University of Lublin.

1956
- December 1. Appointed to the Chair of Ethics at the Catholic University of Lublin.

1958
- July 4. Appointed Auxiliary Bishop to Archbishop Monsigneur Eugeniusz Baziak of Kraków.
- September 28. Ordained as bishop at Wawel Cathedral.

1960
- January. First edition of *Love and Responsibility*. Dissertation, "Building a System of Christian Ethics on the Basis of Max Scheler's Philosophy" published by the Catholic University of Lublin.

1962
- October 11–December 8. Participates in second session of the Second Vatican Council in Rome.
- December 30. Appointed Metropolitan Bishop of Kraków.

1964
- January 13. Appointed Archbishop of Kraków; March 8. Installation ceremony.
- September. Participates in the third session of the Second Vatican Council.

1965
- January 31–April 6. Participates in the work on *Gaudium et Spes*, Vatican II's Pastoral Constitution on the Church in the Contemporary World.
- September 14. Opening of the fourth session of the Second Vatican Council.
- December 8. Closing of the Second Vatican Council.

1966
- December 29. Archbishop Wojtyla is made President of the Episcopal Commission for the Apostolate of the Laity.

1967
- May 29. Named Cardinal by Pope Paul VI.
- June 28. Consecrated Cardinal in the Sistine Chapel.

1968
- December. As Cardinal, attends ceremonies in 120 parishes during visitation of the Black Madonna of Częstochowa.

1969
- The Polish Theological Society of Kraków publishes Cardinal Wojtyla's anthropological work, *The Acting Person*.

1971
- October 5. Elected to the Council of the Secretary General of the Synod of Bishops.

1972
- May 8. Publishes *Foundations of Renewal: A Study on the Implementation of the Second Vatican Council*, which reflects efforts to educate people of his archdiocese on Vatican II.

1975

- February 27. Delivers a paper, "Participation or Alienation?," at an international study seminar in phenomenology in Fribourg, Switzerland.

1976

- March 7–13. Gives spiritual exercises at Vatican, the meditations from which have been published as *A Sign of Contradiction*.

1977

- March 1–15 Receives a doctorate *honoris causa* from Johannes Guttenberg University, Mainz, Germany.

1978

- August 26. John Paul I (Albino Luciani) is elected Pope.
- September 28. Pope John Paul I dies.
- October 3–4. Leaves for the funeral of Pope John Paul I.
- October 14. Conclave begins.
- October 16. Cardinal Karol Wojtyla is elected 263rd Successor of Peter at approximately 5:15 P.M.

1979

- January 24. Accepts request to act as mediator in the border conflict between Argentina and Chile; audience granted to the Soviet Foreign Minister, Andrei Gromyko.
- January 25. Embarks on first pastoral visit outside Italy: to Dominican Republic, Mexico, and the Bahamas.
- March 15. Publication of first papal encyclical: *Redemptor Hominis* (On the Redemption and Dignity of the Human Race).
- June 2–10. Second pastoral visit outside Italy: to Poland.
- September 29–October 8. Third pastoral visit outside Italy: to Ireland and the United States of America.
- October 2. Addresses the General Assembly of the United Nations in New York.
- November 28–30. Fourth pastoral visit outside Italy: to Turkey.

1980

- April 4. Hears Good Friday confessions of the faithful for the first time in St. Peter's Basilica.
- May 2–12. Fifth pastoral visit outside Italy: to Zaire, the Republic of the Congo, Kenya, Ghana, Upper Volta, the Ivory Coast.
- May 30–June 2. Sixth pastoral visit outside Italy: to France.
- June 2. Delivers address to UNESCO in Paris.
- June 21. Receives President Jimmy Carter of the United States.
- June 30–July 12. Seventh pastoral visit outside Italy: to Brazil.
- October 17. Official visits of H.M. Queen Elizabeth II of Great Britain and H.R.H. Prince Philip, Duke of Edinburgh.
- November 15–19. Eighth pastoral visit outside Italy: to West Germany.

- December 2. Publication of second papal encyclical: *Dives in Misericordia* (On the Mercy of God).
- December 19. Official visit of President Cviyetin Mijatovic of the Socialist Federal Republic of Yugoslavia.
- December 30. Apostolic Letter proclaiming Sts. Cyril and Methodius, together with St. Benedict, Patrons of Europe.

1981

- January 15. Receives in audience a delegation of the Polish Independent Syndicate *Solidarnosc*, headed by Lech Walesa.
- February 8. Meets with Rome's Chief Rabbi Elio Toaff.
- February 16–27. Ninth pastoral visit outside Italy: to Pakistan, the Philippines, Guam (USA), Japan, and Anchorage, Alaska.
- May 13. At 5:19 P.M., Turkish terrorist Mehmet Ali Agca makes attempt on the Pope's life. Hospitalized for seventy-seven days at Gemelli hospital.
- May 18. Recites the Angelus at Gemelli hospital: "I am praying for the brother who wounded me and whom I sincerely forgive."
- September 14. Publication of third papal encyclical: *Laborem Exercens* (On Human Work).
- December 12. Sends delegates of the Pontifical Academy of Sciences to presidents of the USA, USSR, Great Britain, France, and to the UN, to explain document on consequences of the use of nuclear arms in Europe and the world.

1982

- February 12–19. Tenth pastoral visit outside Italy: to Nigeria, Benin, Gabon, and Equatorial Guinea.
- May 12–15. Eleventh pastoral visit outside Italy (one year after assassination attempt in St. Peter's Square): to Portugal.
- May 28–June 2. Twelfth pastoral visit outside Italy: to Great Britain.
- May 29. Joint statement with Archbishop of Canterbury, Dr. Robert Runcie, at close of ecumenical celebration in Anglican Canterbury Cathedral.
- June 7. Meets with U.S. President Ronald Reagan for the first time; they pledge to work for world peace and justice.
- June 10–13. Thirteenth pastoral visit outside Italy: to Argentina, in relation to Falkland Islands war between Argentina and Great Britain.
- June 15. Fourteenth pastoral visit outside Italy: to Geneva, Switzerland; speaks at sixty-eighth session of the International Workers Conference.
- August 29. Fifteenth pastoral visit outside Italy: to San Marino and Rimini.
- September 15. Private meeting with President of the Palestinian Liberation Organization Yasser Arafat on prospects for peace in Middle East; renewed appeal for peace in Lebanon following the murder of president-elect Bechir Gemayel.

- October 10. Canonization of Fr. Maximilian Kolbe. Present at the canonization ceremony was Mr. Franciszek Gajownizek, the man for whom Fr. Maximilian offered his life in Auschwitz concentration camp.
- October 31–November 9. Sixteenth pastoral visit outside Italy: to Spain.

1983

- March 2–10. Seventeenth pastoral visit outside Italy: to Portugal and to Central America: Costa Rica, Nicaragua, Panama, El Salvador, Guatemala, Honduras, Belize, and Haiti.
- June 16–23. Eighteenth pastoral visit outside Italy: to Poland.
- August 14. Nineteenth pastoral visit outside Italy: to France.
- September 10–13. Twentieth pastoral visit outside Italy: to Austria.
- October 16. Performs act of consecration of the world to Our Lady of Fatima, together with the cardinals and bishops participating in the Synod of Bishops.
- November 5. Letter for the five hundredth anniversary of the birth of Martin Luther.
- December 11. Meeting with Evangelic-Lutheran community in Rome.
- December 27. Visit with Ali Agca, who had made the May 13, 1981, attempt on his life, in Rebibbia prison.

1984

- January 10. Diplomatic relations between the Holy See and the United States of America.
- March 25. In spiritual union with all the bishops of the world, John Paul II repeats the act of entrustment of mankind and all peoples to Mary Most Holy, at Fatima, Portugal.
- April 20. Apostolic Letter *Redemptionis Anno*, on the city of Jerusalem, sacred patrimony of all believers and crossroads of peace for the peoples of the Middle East.
- May 1. Apostolic Letter *Les Grands Mystères* (on the problem of Lebanon).
- May 2–12. Twenty-first pastoral visit outside Italy: to Korea, Papua New Guinea, the Solomon Islands, and Thailand.
- May 21. Official visit of Italian President Sandro Pertini.
- June 12–17. Twenty-second pastoral visit outside Italy: to Switzerland.
- September 9–20. Twenty-third pastoral visit outside Italy: to Canada.
- October 10–13. Twenty-fourth pastoral visit outside Italy: to Zaragoza, Spain, Santo Domingo, Dominican Republic, and San Juan, Puerto Rico.
- December 11. Publication of the Post-Synodal Pastoral Exhortation, *Reconciliatio and Poenitentia* (Reconciliation and Penance).

1985

- January 26–February 6. Twenty-fifth pastoral visit outside Italy: to Venezuela, Ecuador, Peru, and Trinidad and Tobago.
- May 11–21. Twenty-sixth pastoral visit outside Italy: to the Netherlands, Luxembourg, and Belgium.
- July 2. Publication of fourth papal encyclical: *Slavorum Apostoli* (Apostles of the Slavs).
- August 8–19. Twenty-seventh pastoral visit outside Italy: to Togo, the Ivory Coast, Cameroon, the Republic of Central Africa, Zaire, Kenya, and Morocco.
- September 8. Twenty-eighth pastoral visit outside Italy: to Switzerland and Liechtenstein.
- November 17. Personal message to American and Soviet leaders, Ronald Reagan and Mikhail Gorbachev, for the Geneva summit.

1986

- January 31–February 10. Twenty-ninth pastoral visit outside Italy: to India.
- February 19. Private audience with President Amin Gemayel of Lebanon.
- April 13. Visit to Rome's main synagogue.
- May 30. Publication of fifth papal encyclical: *Dominum et Vivificantem* (On the Holy Spirit).
- July 1–8. Thirtieth pastoral visit outside Italy: to Colombia and Santa Lucia.
- October 4–7. Thirty-first pastoral visit outside Italy: to France.
- October 27. Attends the First World Day of Prayer for Peace, convoked in Assisi, Italy.
- November 18–December 1. Thirty-second pastoral visit outside Italy: to Bangladesh, Singapore, Fiji Islands, New Zealand, Australia, and the Seychelles.

1987

- January 13. Audience with President of the Council of the People's Republic of Poland, General Wojciech Jaruzelski.
- March 25. Publication of sixth papal encyclical: *Redemptoris Mater* (Mother of the Redeemer).
- March 31–April 13. Thirty-third pastoral visit outside Italy: to Uruguay, Chile, and Argentina.
- April 30–May 4. Thirty-fourth pastoral visit outside Italy: to the Federal Republic of Germany.
- June 6. Official visit of President Ronald Reagan of the United States.
- June 8–14. Thirty-fifth pastoral visit outside Italy: to Poland.
- June 25. Official visit of President Kurt Waldheim of the Federal Republic of Austria.
- September 10–21. Thirty-sixth pastoral visit outside Italy: to Canada and the United States; in San Francisco, meets with AIDS patients at Mission Dolores Basilica.
- December 3–7. Visit from His Holiness Dimitrios, Ecumenical Patriarch of Constantinople. Signing of common declaration.
- December 11. Official visit of President Raul Ricardo Alfonsin of the Republic of Argentina.

1988

- February 19. Publication of seventh papal encyclical: *Sollicitudo Rei Socialis* (On Social Concerns).
- May 7–19. Thirty-seventh pastoral visit outside Italy: to Uruguay, Bolivia, Paraguay, and Lima, Peru.
- June 18. Official visit of President Corazon C. Aquino of the Philippines.
- June 23–27. Thirty-eighth pastoral visit outside Italy: to Austria.
- September 10–20. Thirty-ninth pastoral visit outside Italy: to Zimbabwe, Botswana, Lesotho, Mozambique, and Swaziland.
- September 30. Publication of the Apostolic Letter *Mulieris Dignitatem* (On the Dignity and Vocation of Women).
- October 8–11. Fortieth pastoral visit outside Italy: to the European Institutions of Strasbourg and to dioceses of Strasbourg, Metz, and Nancy, in France.

1989

- April 20. Official visit of President Patrick J. Hillery of Ireland.
- April 28–May 6. Forty-first pastoral visit outside Italy: to Madagascar, La Réunion, Zambia, and Malawi.
- June 1–10. Forty-second pastoral trip outside Italy: to Norway, Iceland, Finland, Denmark, and Sweden.
- August 19–21. Forty-third pastoral visit outside Italy: to Santiago de Compostela for the fourth World Youth Day.
- August 27. Apostolic Letter for the fiftieth anniversary of the beginning of the Second World War.
- September 7. Apostolic Letter to all Bishops of the Catholic Church on the situation in Lebanon. World Day of Prayer for Peace in Lebanon.
- September 29–October 2. Official visit of Archbishop of Canterbury, Robert Runcie. Signing of common declaration.
- October 6–10. Forty-fourth pastoral visit outside Italy: to Korea, Indonesia, and Mauritius.
- December 1. Official visit of President Mikhail Gorbachev of the USSR.

1990

- January 25–February 1. Forty-fifth pastoral visit outside Italy: to Cape Verde, Guinea-Bissau, Mali, Burkina Faso, and Chad.
- April 21–22. Forty-sixth pastoral visit outside Italy: to Czechoslovakia.
- April 27. Official visit of President Mario Soares of Portugal.
- May 6–14. Forty-seventh pastoral visit outside Italy: to Mexico and Curaçao.
- May 25–27. Forty-eighth pastoral visit outside Italy: to Malta.
- August 26. Papal appeal for peace in the Persian Gulf following invasion of Kuwait by Iraq.
- September 1–10. Forty-ninth pastoral visit outside Italy: to Tanzania, Burundi, Rwanda, and the Ivory Coast.
- December 25. Message taken from the Holy Father's Christmas *Urbi et Orbi*: an appeal for peace in the Persian Gulf.

1991

- January 15. In an attempt to avert the Gulf War, letters sent to U.S. President George Bush and to President Saddam Hussein of Iraq.
- January 22. Publication of eighth papal encyclical: *Redemptoris missio* (On the Permanent Validity of the Church's Missionary Mandate)
- March 4–5. Meeting at Vatican of episcopal representatives from countries directly implicated in the Gulf War.
- April 22. Official visit of the President of the Republic of Chile, Patricio Aylwuin Azocar.
- May 1. Publication of ninth papal encyclical: *Centesimus Annus* (The Hundredth Year).
- May 10–13. Fiftieth pastoral visit outside Italy: to Portugal.
- June 1–9. Fifty-first pastoral visit outside Italy: to Poland.
- August 13–20. Fifty-second pastoral visit outside Italy: to Poland, for the sixth World Youth Day.
- October 5. Ecumenical prayer service at St. Peter's Basilica, on occasion of the sixth centenary of the canonization of St. Brigit of Sweden. For the first time since the Reformation two Lutheran bishops prayed in St. Peter's Basilica with the Pope, together with the Catholic bishops of Stockholm and Helsinki.
- October 12–21. Fifty-third pastoral visit outside Italy: to Brazil.

1992

- January 1. Holy See recognizes Russian Federation.
- February 8. Diplomatic relations with Croatia, Slovenia, and Ukraine.
- February 19–26. Fifty-fourth pastoral visit outside Italy: to Senegal, Gambia, and Guinea.
- June 4–10. Fifty-fifth pastoral visit outside Italy: to Angola and São Tomé and Principe.
- August 22. Dramatic appeal for peace in the Balkans during Angelus message.
- October 9–14. Fifty-sixth pastoral visit outside Italy: to Dominican Republic.
- November 27. Official visit of President Oscar Luigi Scalfaro of the Italian Republic.
- December 7. Papal presentation of Catechism of the Catholic Church to representatives from the Roman Curia and to the presidents of doctrinal and catechismal commissions of Episcopal Conferences.

1993

- January 9. Start of special prayer meeting in Assisi, Italy, for peace in Europe, particularly in the Balkans.
- February 3–10. Fifty-seventh pastoral visit outside Italy: to Benin, Uganda, and Sudan.
- April 25. Fifty-eighth pastoral visit outside Italy: to Albania.
- June 12–17. Fifty-ninth pastoral visit outside Italy: to Spain.
- August 6. Tenth papal encyclical: *Veritatis Splendor* (The Splendor of Truth), published October 5, 1993.
- August 9–16. Sixtieth pastoral visit outside Italy: to Jamaica, Merida Venezuela and to Denver, Colorado, USA, for the celebration of the eighth World Youth Day.

- September 4–10. Sixty-first pastoral visit outside Italy: to Lithuania, Latvia, and Estonia.
- December 16. Official visit of President Carlos Saul Menem of Argentina.
- December 30. Signing of accord on basic principles regulating diplomatic relations between the Holy See and Israel.

1994
- January 23. Papal mass in St. Peter's Basilica for peace in the Balkans.
- March 3. Official visit of President Richard von Weizsäcker of the Federal Republic of Germany; diplomatic relations with the Hashemite Kingdom of Jordan.
- March 5. Diplomatic relations with the Republic of South Africa.
- March 7. Official visit of President Vaclav Havel of the Czech Republic.
- March 17. Official visit from Israeli Prime Minister Yitzhak Rabin.
- April 7. Vatican concert for the commemoration of the Shoah, in the presence of Chief Rabbi of Rome, Elio Toaff.
- September 5–13. Holy See sends delegation to International Conference on Population and Development, held in Cairo, Egypt.
- September 10–11. Sixty-second pastoral visit outside Italy: to Zagreb, Croatia.
- October 20. Publication of Pope John Paul's book *Crossing the Threshold of Hope*.
- December 13. Letter to Children in the Year of the Family.

1995
- January 11–21. Sixty-third pastoral visit outside Italy: to Manila, Philippines, for the celebration of the tenth World Youth Day, and to Port Moresby (Papua New Guinea), Sydney, Australia, and Colombo, Sri Lanka.
- March 6–12. Holy See sends its delegation to the seven-day United Nations World Summit of Social Development in Copenhagen, Denmark.
- March 25. Eleventh papal encyclical: *Evangelium Vitae* (The Gospel of Life), published March 30.
- May 20–22. Sixty-fourth pastoral visit outside Italy: to Czech Republic.
- May 30. Publication of twelfth papal encyclical: *Ut Unim Sint* (That All May Be One).
- June 3–4. Sixty-fifth pastoral visit outside Italy: to Belgium.
- June 27–30. Visit of Ecumenical Patriarch of Constantinople Bartolomeo I; common declaration signed on June 29.
- June 29. Letter to Women, published July 10.
- June 30–July 3. Sixty-sixth pastoral visit outside Italy: to Slovak Republic.
- September 4–15. Appoints Dr. Mary Ann Glendon to head a Holy See delegation and address the fourth United Nations Conference on Women in Beijing, China.

- September 14–20. Sixty-seventh pastoral visit outside Italy: to Yaoundé, Cameroon, Johannesburg and Pretoria, South Africa, and Nairobi, Kenya, for the conclusion of the Special Assembly for Africa of the Synod of Bishops.
- October 4–9. Sixty-eighth pastoral visit outside Italy: to New York, Newark, and Baltimore, in the United States. His foreign trips now have reached the one-million-kilometer mark.
- October 5. Addresses UN General Assembly, commemorates United Nations' fiftieth anniversary.

1996
- February 5–12. Sixty-ninth pastoral visit outside Italy: to Guatemala, Nicaragua, El Salvador, and Venezuela.
- April 14. Seventieth pastoral visit outside Italy: to Tunisia.
- May 17–19. Seventy-first pastoral visit outside Italy: to Slovenia.
- June 3–14. Holy See sends delegation to Habitat II, the UN II Conference on Human Settlements: in Istanbul.
- June 21–23. Seventy-second pastoral visit outside Italy: to Germany; historical speech at gate of Brandenburg, and announcement of the new Synod for Europe.
- September 6–7. Seventy-third pastoral visit outside Italy: to Hungary.
- September 19–22. Seventy-fourth pastoral visit outside Italy: to France.
- November 13. Addresses the opening of the UN World Food Summit organized by the United Nations' Food and Agricultural Organization (FAO) in Rome.
- November 15. Presentation of the Holy Father's book *Gift and Mystery: On the Fiftieth Anniversary of My Priestly Ordination*.
- November 19. Receives in a private visit Dr. Fidel Castro Ruz, President of the Council of State and the Council of Ministers of the Republic of Cuba.
- December 3–6. Visit from Archbishop of Canterbury and Primate of the Anglican Communion, His Grace Dr. George Leonard Carey; signing of common declaration.
- December 10–14. Receives the Supreme Patriarch and Catholicos of all Armenians, His Holiness Karekin I; signing of common declaration.

1997
- January 23–26. Visit from His Holiness Aram I Keshishian, Catholicos of Cilicia of the Armenians; signing of common declaration.
- February 3. Receives Israeli Prime Minister, Benjamin Netanyahu.
- February 14. Official visit of Brazilian President, Fernando Henrique Cardoso.
- March 10. Holy See and Libya establish Diplomatic Relations.
- April 7. Audience granted to President of Poland, Aleksander Kwasniewski.
- April 12–13. Seventy-fifth pastoral visit outside Italy: to Sarajevo.

- April 25–27. Seventy-sixth pastoral visit outside Italy: to the Czech Republic, on the occasion of the one thousandth anniversary of the death of St. Adalbert.
- May 10–11. Seventy-seventh pastoral visit outside of Italy: to Beirut, for concluding phase of the Special Assembly for Lebanon of the Synod of Bishops.
- May 16. Receives President of Georgia, Eduard Shevardnadze.
- May 31–June 10. Seventy-eighth pastoral visit outside Italy: to Poland.
- June 16. Letters written to Benjamin Netanyahu, Prime Minister of Israel, and to Yasser Arafat, President of the Palestinian National Authority, regarding the Middle East peace process.
- June 24. Letter to President Boris N. Yeltsin of the Russian Federation, on Religious Freedom.
- August 21. Seventy-ninth pastoral visit outside Italy: to Paris, for the celebration of the twelfth World Youth Day.
- October 19. Eightieth pastoral visit outside Italy: to Brazil.

1998
- January 21–26. Eighty-first pastoral visit outside Italy: to the Republic of Cuba and a meeting with Cuban President Fidel Castro Ruz.
- March 7. Receives Madeleine Albright, Secretary of State for the United States of America.
- March 13–21. Eighty-third pastoral visit outside Italy: to Austria.
- March 21–23. Eighty-second pastoral visit outside Italy: to Nigeria.
- May 15. Audience with their Majesties King Alberto II and Queen Paola of Belgium.
- June 12. Receives Yasser Arafat, President of the Palestinian National Authority.
- June 18. Audience with the President of the Republic of South Africa, Nelson Mandela.
- June 19–21. Eighty-fourth pastoral visit outside Italy: to Croatia.

1999
- January 8. Audience with the Prime Minister of the Italian Republic, Massimo D'Alema.
- January 22–27. Eighty-fifth pastoral visit outside Italy: to Mexico City, Mexico, and St. Louis, Missouri, USA.

Bibliography

Bernstein, Carl, and Marco Politi. *His Holiness*. New York: Doubleday, 1996.

Buell, Raymond Leslie. *Poland: The Key to Europe*. New York: Alfred A. Knopf, 1939.

Coleman, Fred. *The Decline and Fall of the Soviet Empire*. New York: St. Martin's Press, 1996.

Craig, Mary. *Man from a Far Country: An Informal Portrait of Pope John Paul II*. New York: Morrow, 1979.

Gorbachev, Mikhail. *Memoirs*. New York: Doubleday, 1995.

Halecki, O. *A History of Poland*. New York: Roy Publishers. 1943.

Hardon, John A., Editor. *The Treasury of Catholic Wisdom*. San Francisco: Ignatius Press, 1987.

His Holiness John Paul II. *Crossing the Threshold of Hope*. New York: Alfred A. Knopf, 1994.

His Holiness Pope John Paul II. *Gift and Mystery*. New York: Doubleday, 1996.

Issacs, Jeremy and Downing, Taylor. *Cold War : An Illustrated History, 1945–1991*. Boston: Little Brown, 1998.

Kwitny, Jonathan. *Man of the Century: The Life and Times of Pope John Paul II*. New York: Henry Holt and Co, 1997.

Lukas, Richard C. *The Forgotten Holocaust*. Lexington: The University Press of Kentucky,1986.

Malinski, Lieczyslaw. *Pope John Paul II: The Life of Karol Wojtyla*. New York: The Seabury Press, 1979.

O' Brien, Darcy. *The Hidden Pope*. New York: Daybreak Books, 1998.

Peterkiewicz, Jerzy (Translator). *The Place Within: The Poetry of Pope John Paul II*. New York: Random House, 1982.

Pietritangeli, Carlo, et al. *The Sistine Chapel*. New York: Harmony Books, 1986.

Steven, Stewart. *The Poles*. New York: Macmillan Publishing Co., Inc., 1982.

Syrop, Konrad. *Poland: Between the Hammer and the Anvil*. London: Robert Hale, Great Britain. 1968.

Szulc, Tad. *Pope John Paul II: The Biography*. Scribner. New York: 1995.

Van Norman, Louis E. *Poland: The Knight Among Nations*. New York: Fleming H. Revell Co. 1907.

Walsh, Meg Nottingham. "Out of the Darkness: Michelangelo's Last Judgment." *National Geographic*, May 1994, pp. 102-22.

Weschler, Lawrence. *Passion of Poland*. New York: Pantheon Books, 1984.

Whale, John (Editor). *The Man Who Leads the Church: An Assessment of Pope John Paul II*. San Francisco: Harper and Row Publishers, 1980.

Wojtyla, Karol Josef. *The Collected Plays and Writings on Theater*. Np: University of California Press, 1987.

Wright, Robin. "What Would the World Be Like Without Him?" *The Atlantic Monthly*, July 1994.

Wynn, Wilton. *Keepers of the Keys*. New York: Random House, 1988.

Photo Credits

Index

Index